Youth
Considers
"Do-It-Yourself"
Religion

YOUTH FORUM SERIES

Titles in Print

Youth Asks, Why Bother About God?
  by Alvin N. Rogness
Youth Considers Sex
  by William E. Hulme
Youth Considers "Do-It-Yourself" Religion
  by Martin E. Marty

Titles in Preparation

Youth Considers the World of High School
  by John S. Wood
Youth Considers Life Goals
  by Ross Snyder
Youth Considers Personal Moods
  by Reuel L. Howe
Youth Considers Parental Authority
  by Randolph C. Miller
Youth Considers Doubt and Frustration
  by Paul L. Holmer

Youth
Considers
"DO-IT-YOURSELF"
RELIGION

by
Martin E. Marty

THOMAS NELSON & SONS

London   NEW YORK   *Toronto*

Foreword

Written in the context of the Christian faith, this book is one in a series published by Thomas Nelson & Sons in collaboration with Church Youth Research.

The research agency, which serves as editor of this series, is known through *What Youth Are Thinking* (Smedsrud, 1961) and *Profiles of Church Youth* (Strommen, 1963). The Director, Dr. Merton Strommen, is known also for his work as Director of Research (1965-67) with Religious Education Association, an inter-faith agency serving all church groups.

The purpose of the series is to use points of established need to bring about meaningful contact between the GOSPEL of God in Jesus Christ and YOUNG PEOPLE. Underlying the total effort is a concern that youth throughout the English-speaking world can be helped to see that the Gospel of Christ is the core of life itself in all its realities.

Unique to this publication effort is the use that is made of research findings. These describe the specific need to which each book is addressed as well as the youth most concerned about this need. Thus a writer is helped to speak more directly to the actual conflicts, values, and beliefs of an important segment of youth.

The significance of this series is enhanced by the scholarship and pastoral concern of the authors. Their grasp of the fields in which each writes enables them to speak with authority, establishing the series as a basic reference in the area of youth work.

Preface

One of the problems that a teacher faces in trying to present Christianity to modern young people is that they think they already know all about the religion. It is an old-hat religion, one that was suitable perhaps for the Middle Ages, the Renaissance, or even the nineteenth century but one that is hardly suitable for the present. Christianity is a religion that has been tried once and tried several times and found wanting.

The dedicated Christian is somewhat at a loss as to explain how Christianity could ever have become trite. The Gospels are revolutionary documents with revolutionary content that would appear as dangerous to a conservative visitor from Mars as it appeared to the conservative enemies of Jesus in the first century. Unfortunately, the revolutionary nature of the gospel story has become obscured by familiarity. It just does not seem that notions we have heard all of our life can possibly have much in the way of dynamic relevance for contemporary problems.

The truth of the matter, of course, is not that Christianity has been tried and found wanting but, as Gilbert Chesterton put it, it has been found hard and not tried. The "religion in general" which Dr. Marty describes in the present book is a watered-down version of Christianity that is often confused with the real product. The Christianity that young people are frequently tempted to reject is a comfortable, pious, empty kind of faith that may in some instances bring a soothing peace of soul in times of worry and anxiety but it is hardly likely to provide much of a dynamic vision which a young person is seeking for his life.

There may be some young people who are content with a captive religion, with a religion that makes no demands on either their faith or morality and requires little in the way of dedication to the social problems of the world around them. But the élite young people of our society, the young men and women who see visions are seeking for something much different. They are looking for a religion that is challenging, a religion that makes heavy demands on them, a religion that has vigorous comments to make on the social problems which face the world. Dr. Marty suggests in this volume that such a religion is traditional Christianity, not the traditional "religion in general" which we have come to think of as Christianity but rather the authentic Christianity of the Gospels. He suggests that revolutionary young people who are looking for an exciting and challenging faith should at least investigate the real Christianity; and that they should judge Christianity by what it really is and not by what the purveyors of its comfortable counterfeit would have us believe it is.

He does not argue that this authentic gospel Christianity is for everyone. But he does seem to suggest that any young person who is interested in a systematic investigation on the various faiths on which he may build his life should look at authentic Christianity and should be able to fully distinguish between authentic Christianity and the synthetic "religion in general."

Dr. Marty is arguing that heresy comes easy, that in Orthodox faith there is real challenge and real excitement. Such an argument will fall on unsympathetic ears among those who have tried to reduce the gospel to a series of harmless and vague propositions. It will also, however, provide material for serious thought among that crucial group of young people who are not content with pat answers or easy solutions.

Andrew M. Greeley

University of Chicago

Contents

Introduction

"Pull up a chair. Let's talk." I feel strange, beginning a book so personally. Historians and theologians, whose company I keep, are trained to be reserved and detached, to be almost impersonal in their writings. But I am told that my subject will be best introduced if I envision myself in the gathering of serious young people who are taking up a serious topic. They are giving me the opportunity to introduce any subject which might be of interest to me, and I begin.

Pull up a chair. What shall we talk about? I know that your topics often deal with problems of your own age group. You talk about dating and mating and finding jobs. But I know that more and more younger people are trying to relate to a larger world and they are forced sooner than their parents were into taking sides on issues affecting the whole society. One of these which interests me is the American Way of Life or, more precisely, the temptation Americans have to worship and idolize their way of life.

Whenever people come together in a very complicated society they look for uniting simplicities. We have hundreds of ideas about political life, but almost all of us assent to a general set of beliefs as expressed in our Declaration of Independence or the Preamble to the Constitution. Canadians have the same problem with the American Way of Life, by the way. I am not speaking only about the United States. Canadians have different documents, but again theirs is a religiously free society and their uniting beliefs are basically political.

Religiously also we are a very complicated society. They

tell us that over 250 religious groups compete for national attention and at least ten large families of denominations are bidding for us to hear. If we listen to all, we fall into chaos and anarchy. If we listen only to one, we devise a religious monopoly. So we pick and choose. We get a bit of belief here and a bit of faith there; we put together a religion of sorts based on the memories of Christianity, the ideas behind our politics, and anything else that happens to please us. I want to describe that process and will call its result "religion-in-general." Many refer to it as "do-it-yourself religion" but in either case they mean the same thing.

I believe we can discern in America an impulse and even a vague set of beliefs which are commonly held. Maybe a society needs them and they can be productive. But such beliefs can also be "household gods." We put them together; they give us happiness and comfort because we can control them. We cannot always control the inherited religions as we can control those we devise.

Since I am talking about the culture-religion developed on our shores, some of what I say may sound a bit subversive. Here let me say that we ought to get acquainted. Really, I find many attractive features in our way of life. Whenever I return to America from a foreign trip I am almost ready to kiss the soil. I usually settle for saluting the flag and ordering an American hamburger and milk shake. I am moved by the ceremonies of state. My investment in America's economy and future is apparent, if shaky: I hold a dozen credit cards, a mortgage with eighteen years to go on a house and adjoining pool—which proves I am corruptible—and own two aging automobiles. To my knowledge I am not on any Attorney-General's subversive lists.

But I want to be subversive. I want help, and I want to

give help, so that none of us may fall into the trap of taking a way of life and idolizing it. The fine line between having loyalty to a set of institutions and worshiping them needs new detailing in every generation. Ours is not the first society in which people have devised culture-religions. But we have to think through the problem of what is original in our own time, and then we have to find ways of separating loyalty from idolatry.

To do this, I propose to try three simple things in this book. First, we shall try to define what it takes for a belief-system or attitude to come to be called religious. That means we will have to talk about religion in a general way. Then, we shall try to account for our culture's "religion-in-general" and to see what positive features are in it. Third, I shall try to provide guidelines for examining and criticizing such a religion. This book is written from the viewpoint of distinctive Christianity, a Christianity which can and does contribute to national life but which is ill-served and serves ill if it is absorbed in a general national religion and lets itself become a mere servant of the state.

One would not need to be a Christian to write most of this book. A Jew, for example, could share concern about being absorbed or swallowed up in a generalized religion. People of other religions also might feel that society should be judged by standards "revealed" to it or coming from outside it and not by standards which are produced by it. But I am interested in the Christian future and write from that viewpoint. I am not pretending that Christian churches are perfect and thus that they always have a right to judge the society. They have to be judged first. Many of the problems described in this book are strongest problems inside the churches. "We have faults we haven't even used yet." But churches speak in the name of a Lord who does stand above and beyond national purpose and above and beyond our household gods. I should think that if we invoke His name and presence, we would want to listen to Him.

Now, I will try to stay out of the way of the plot.

What we know in general about religion

RELIGION: A WELL-WORN WORD

The word "religion" is so familiar that it hardly needs explanation. Every mature person has occasion to use it quite frequently. The best way to come to an understanding of its meanings is to test some of its common usages.

WHO ARE RELIGIOUS PEOPLE?

What do we mean by the adjective when we say, "He's so religious"? As soon as we hear the word, some picture or other comes to mind. More often than not, it may be a picture which indicates that we naturally react against a religious person. This must mean that in our minds it is possible that religion can become a bad thing, if it produces distasteful people.

In his book for children, *Ounce Dice Trice*, the poet Alastair Reid has provided some "odd words, either forgotten or undiscovered, with which you can bamboozle almost anyone." One of these undiscovered words is "Mim." Reid defines the adjective by applying it: "What are Mim People? Mim people are very proper people who always sit

15

with their fingertips together and their lips pursed tight,
who always do the right thing and who always disapprove." [1]

The illustrator, Ben Shahn, has provided a drawing of
a "mim" man which stamps the picture in our mind. A
mim person is almost always religious: he always does the
right thing, and always disapproves. "He's *so* religious!" Of
whom do we think? There was that third assistant to the
Sunday School principal who used to wait in the hall for
any child to show a sign of humanness. Then our mim religious friend would disapprove. "She's *so* religious!" We
think of the pale, blue-veined girl back in grade school, the
one who kept up good communications with the teacher.
She applied her high standards to our conduct and when
we failed, she reported. She could afford to have high standards; no one liked her anyhow.

Somehow the picture of frustrated, joyless, disapproving
people comes to mind when we hear of a religious person.
We know we are supposed to model ourselves after religious people, and sometimes feel guilty if we fail and even
guiltier if we do not try. No one has made quite clear to
anyone else why "very proper people who always sit with
their fingertips together and their lips pursed tight" are
better models than are the hearty, joyful, and outgoing.
But the picture is there and we keep on trying to live up
to it.

WE LIKE SOME RELIGIOUS PEOPLE

At the opposite extreme: we might also apply the adjective to the best and most heroic people we know. We
approve of certain kinds of religious persons. For some un-
explainable reason it seems easier to apply the term "reli-

[1] Boston: Little, Brown & Company, 1958, pp. 43, 52.

gious" to older people than to younger ones. We think of a grandmother who is all alone in the world. Most of the doors of opportunity have closed on her and she is left with memories and mementos. Her lifelong partner is no longer with her and her children have moved. She seems to have little to do but wait. Yet, while waiting, she seems to be open to what each day may bring. She may have suffered much, but she is full of brightness and hope. She may seem to have gotten less than the best end of the deal out of life, yet she turns regularly to her Bible and prayer book and speaks of praise. She is religious and, while we cannot now identify with her or have much occasion to model our lives after hers, we mean it as a compliment to call her religious.

Younger people sometimes deserve and have the term "religious" applied to them. A martyr to Nazism or Communism is someone we much admire. As we read his letters and last messages we are inclined to say that he was religious. An athlete who is able to act on the basis of profound spiritual convictions and who is able to speak of them in the proper circumstances may be religious, in the minds of his friends. It seems as if the adjective means something good or something bad, depending upon whether we had or had not previously admired the one to whom it is applied. In any case, something called religion must have gone into the make-up of both those whom we despise and those whom we admire.

WE APPROVE OR DISAPPROVE

Try the adverb. "He stuck with his hobby religiously." Again, the term can apply approval or disapproval. Perhaps he was obsessed with his collection of fruit-flies or HO-gauge railroad cars. He refined his approach to them so that no one else's collection seemed to amount to anything. He spoke disparagingly of others. He took no interest in anything else in life. "Purity of heart is to will one thing," and he willed only that his collection would grow and his hobby would improve. He was a fanatic, devoted to the worship of fruit-flies or HO-gauge cars. No priest and no devotee of a world religion has spent so much time adoring the object of his religion as did our acquaintance who took his hobby religiously. We disapproved: he was selfish, inverted, grim, joyless. We might like to see his collections, but we honestly had little interest in him.

"Oh, I used to have to go to church religiously when I was a child" is the kind of sentence that is used by an adult who has turned his back on the church. Again, in our minds, a gray picture forms. We see a little child being ribboned and bonneted and being pushed out of the front door or being driven by father. The parent had done nothing to set an example or to explain to the child what was happening. He or she was simply pushed along into the sanctuary and his attitudes were expected to develop. Out of fear or custom or habit the child goes through with the action—what chance has he to avoid it?—and goes to church religiously. It would not occur to him to do anything else. Until he is an adult, when he will look back on a tidy but unhappy world and say, "Oh, when I was a child I used to go to church religiously."

On the other hand, some people seem so selfless, so extroverted, so joyful, and so free to share that we say they live religiously, and we mean thus to congratulate them. "We went to a youth retreat and rededicated ourselves to God. Looking back on that summer week-end I cannot help but think, we had never lived so religiously before." "He didn't care how much fun they made of him, he had the courage to say his prayers religiously."

RELIGION AND RELIGIONS AS CATEGORIES

The adjective and the adverb are both double-sided. People use them both to condemn or to congratulate those to whom they can be applied. This double-sidedness provides a clue to the fact that we had better move on, if we seek understanding, to the noun. What is behind this thing, "religion," that makes it play such a big part in our appraisal of persons?

Immediately, the word gets its user into trouble. As often as not the word refers to something we do not like. The world may have hundreds of religions and we hold to only one of them. This gives us odds of hundreds to one that we will be disagreeing more than we will be agreeing with what people refer to when they speak of religion.

For example, Henry Louis Mencken in his study of the American language asserts that the phrase "to get religion" is uniquely American. It was born here. When someone gets religion he acquires something he did not previously have. The town bum, just coming out of an alcoholic stupor, is probably the best prospect for conversion on the part of the traveling revivalist. The bum turns up in the revivalist's tent and in a torrent of emotion he gets religion. Out pours a record of his guilt, a gush of sentiment, and a packet of resolves. All of them will be forgotten tomorrow. A young man is courting a girl who, with her family, is strongly devoted to the church. He uses all the weapons that are fair in love and war, but her parents ponder his depth of character. Without too much effort, especially for the times when they are looking, he can get religion. He will join something or speak and act in such a way that the show can go on.

Religion need not mean only sham and hypocrisy. In our

culture we seem to have to use the same word to refer to matters which all thoughtful people hold in high regard. A statesman may speak of "our most holy religion," and people who are a bit careless—as we shall see later—may refer to "the religion of Jesus Christ," and we instinctively place a high value on both. To "get religion" may also mean joining a church and experiencing a release and a freedom which was not previously present.

A SUBJECT FOR STUDY

A moment ago it was noted that the world is full of hundreds of religions. When the noun is used in the plural, something else comes to mind. It can refer to a general category of study, a general topic. "Have you studied comparative religion?" means, "Have you compared the religions of men and have you studied the religious impulse?" The comparative study of religion or religions is an exacting science. Experts study tribal dances and totems. They listen to chants and observe conduct and read sacred books. In every instance they are dealing with the general topic of the meaning and place of religion.

"Have you studied your religion?" is a legitimate question for a student in a Christian school to ask another. In such an instance he probably means, "Have you studied your religion course?" and with that question he applies the term to the Christian faith and some information which grows out of it. The word "religion" can be a very general category, or it may be, as it will turn out to be in this book, something quite pointed and specific. Clearly the word is vague and it tells us little; our uses of it are varied, and they do little more than provide us with clues. Whenever a word suffers such a fate or experiences such a destiny, we know that it has been around a long time and has had to mean many things to many people.

THE REASONS FOR VAGUENESS

The word "religion" applies to some antique realities. Some of them are widespread and we have little difficulty in forming impressions concerning them. A religion can refer to hundreds of millions of people, gathered for worship. A German encyclopedia published in 1950 divided the world into religions. At that time there were 775 million people called Christian; 350 million called Muslim; 320 million called Hindu. Our world included 150 million nominal Buddhists, 12 million Jews, 36 million Taoists, 34 million Shintoists, 130 million animists and primitives, and 300 million who had been adherents of the Chinese religions of Confucianism. To round things out, 593 million were regarded as religiously uncommitted. One of the difficulties which we shall experience in discussing religion-in-general is this: it does not appear in the above listing. It has no clear "slice of the pie" among the religions of the world. In our culture it attracts nominal Christians and people otherwise not committed. Yet it is something specific, and, in the forms we know it, something quite new.

If I talk about religion in a general way I am very vague and have not yet come to the subject of this book. If I talk about a specific body of beliefs and attitudes called "religion-in-general" I mean to be specific and to point to something which can be carefully examined. If someone uses the word "weapon" he has not provided us with a clear picture. It is an old and general word which has had to gather up under its cover many newer and more specific meanings. If someone uses the expression, "intercontinental ballistics missile," he provides something clearer. It is new and specific and has not yet had such a history. Readers who have the patience to track down "religion-in-general" will find that we can be quite specific about it, because in our form it is quite new and definable. But because we live in the middle of its development, it can easily elude us.

Vagueness attaches to it because "religion" refers to something very profound. We find it easier to give definition to shallow and specific objects, like "gutter" or "saucer," than to profound and general realities like birth or death or love or even "the boundless sea." Whatever else religion sets out to do, it wants to provide man with a universe of meaning. Little wonder that definition is difficult. Vagueness attaches to it also because "religion" refers to something very broad. An expression like "intercontinental ballistics missile" can clearly apply only to a specific object or a small family of objects while a word like "weapon" applies to many. If nothing like religion had ever occurred in the memory of man, and if now a prophet should arise and invent it, he would have less difficulty than we have, with all our rich inheritance.

Some people contrive and calculate to put vagueness into the term. Such activity can throw others off the trail. One can say he is just using the English language, but he can privately fill it with some Anglo-Saxon four-letter words which would not be approved. One can say, "we were just dancing"; but a dance can mean something sacred, or merely friendly and expressive, or it can mean something obscene and immoral. Apply a general and vague word and fix it in someone's mind, and you are free to be precise and specific while he is thinking about it and not watching you. Call an action religious and you will fix in people's minds a category which they allow. But inside that category devise something like religion-in-general, and they might, after they recover from distraction, be less ready to approve it. For all of these reasons we want to remain properly suspicious of anyone who speaks of "religious" or "religiously," of "religion" or "religions." We shall want to know what is going on inside the categories.

CONFUSION BY DESIGN

By now there must be some readers who feel more confused than when they began. Good. We are trying to create a maze; the act of finding our way out is suppose to inform us and to cause us to think. But there is always some man of action in view who is impatient and who prematurely seeks the simplicity which we shall seek later on. "Don't confuse us with so many meanings. Don't throw us off the trail by reference to other faiths. Everybody knows what religion is; let's content ourself with the usual definition."

We can understand and sympathize with this desire for simplicity. But is it true that everybody knows what religion is? St. Augustine once said, "I always know what time is, until someone asks me." Each of us knows what time is. Can we define it? Try to. It is simple to know what time it is, but not what time is. My dictionary informs me that time is "all the days there have ever been or ever will be; the past, present, and future." Look at your watch: has the definition helped? The dictionary goes on to define time as "a part of time," which does not help me very much. Its third definition is "a period of time; epoch, era." Suppose some being came to our world from a timeless realm and we were asked to explain what "everybody knows" about time.

THE MANY DEFINITIONS

So it is with religion. Not everyone tries to be technical or confusing. They may be trying to be very clear and specific. Everybody knows what religion is. But if we gather a circle of people and someone asks us, we no longer know. "Religion refers to belief in Jesus Christ." It does not. Not at all. There is a religion which has to do with people and institutions who are devoted to Jesus Christ. But neither Christian thinkers nor anti-Christian thinkers will have much to be happy about in the definition. We began too specifically. "Religion is man's attempt to find God." But certainly most Christian people feel that it has to do with God's search for man. All right, "Religion refers to God's activity in the world and to man's response to it." Half the Christian thinkers we know would resist such a definition, and all nonbelievers would reject the idea that God *is* or that God's activity *exists.* "Everybody knows," but none of us really know when we are asked.

TWO ROOTS AND ONE WORD

The same dictionary which confused me on the matter of time does the same with "religion." Its first definitions speak of "belief in God or gods; worship of God or gods." Its latter definitions have to do with "a particular system of belief and worship," or "a matter of conscience." When the dictionary tries to set the word against the background of ancient languages it opens a controversial topic. We read:

> Latin *religio,* respect for what is sacred; probably (originally) care for (worship and traditions), from *re-legere,* go through, or read again; *religio* was apparently strongly influenced, in popular thought, by the verb *re-ligare,* to bind, in the sense, "place an obligation on."

When the authors of a dictionary start using words like "probably" or "apparently" they are admitting that there is uncertainty. In a field so important as this, armies charge through such cracks in doors. Books and libraries are full of debate about the two possible origins in Latin of the word "religion." The debate is not unimportant.

If "religion" comes from and refers to *relegere,* with its sense of what man has respect for as sacred, the emphasis is "objective"; it concentrates on the object or goal of religion. If it comes from *religare,* with its sense of how man is bound by obligation, the emphasis is "subjective"; it concentrates on the subject or agent of religion. One can see how dramatic this difference is. One accents God, the other accents man. One turns outward, the other turns inward.

Fortunately, this is not the place to detail the controversies. We can only cite them. Recently some scholars have suggested ways out of the debate. Wilfred Cantwell Smith in a book, *The Meaning and End of Religion,* contends that two roots or even two original words have come together to form the term. He does not want to have us decide between religion as referring to the object or religion as referring to the subject: they complement each other. Another scholar suggests that neither of the two Latin words discussed were at the original root, but rather a word which meant "to pay attention to, to give care." No one really knows.

THE SUBJECT OF RELIGION

Whatever we want to say about religion, we want to remember for a discussion of religion-in-general. In the discussion of the root of the word itself, we shall lean toward a usage which stresses the subject and not the object, the agent of religion and not the goal. Religion-in-general is generally vague about what (or Who) it has respect for as being sacred; it concerns itself more with the man "bound" by obligation.

In our quest for an easy definition to pass on to others, we are not helped much by great men who have commented on religion. Each man brings an idea to the subject and then makes the subject fit. Try a few: Matthew Arnold said religion was "morality touched with emotion." But we know of unemotional religions; and, surprising as it may sound, many religions have not only seemed immoral but have not cared about morality. Religion-in-general does happen to speak a great deal more about morality than about emotion.

Alfred North Whitehead said, "religion is what a man does with his solitariness." It is clearly true that profound religious events occur to men when they are alone. But almost all religions define themselves not for people on islands but for people in community. Religion-in-general certainly does, though it allows for solitary worship by a man at the end of a golf club or a fishing rod, or a woman with her ear attuned to a symphonic recording. "Anything that lifts man above the realities of this material life is religion." This was the definition of Max Müller, a great and early student of world religions. A German religous thinker, Friedrich Schleiermacher, called it "a feeling of absolute dependence." In our own time, Paul Tillich speaks of "ultimate concern." We could supply an endless list of such personal definitions. Some of them are better than others; some agree with each other to form clusters or composites while some compete with all others. Once again we must remember: in a subject such as this, the definition will largely grow out of the describer's attitude toward what he describes. So it shall be with our own; we are not likely to escape the problem.

TRY YOUR OWN DEFINITION

When trying to form your definition, let other people test you. Here are some examples:

"Religion is all about God." If so, what about forms of

Buddhism which are a-theistic? That is, it is part of the religion to assert that there is no God.

"Religion is all about how man holds onto meaning." If so, what about the classic Christian thinkers, who say that man counts for little or nothing in their faith? Their faith is all about how God holds onto man.

"Religion is an academic study." That is, one can take courses on it in a high school or college. But most people who adhere to religion want it to be anything but academic and are probably mistrustful or resentful of scholars and students or critics.

"Religion refers to the faiths men live by." But a great many men and women of faith want to be "open to God." By their definition, religion is the opposite term to faith. To them it means being closed to God because one is preoccupied with what one brings Him in the way of piety, attitude, or philosophy. To them "religion" and "faith" stand against each other; they can never be synonyms.

"Religion refers to *my* beliefs." If so, how are you going to rule out what everyone else believes?

SHAKING OUR FOUNDATIONS

We all know people who believe that the way to find truth is to be pacific. They are weary of argument. They resent careful definition. They do not want the planks and stones turned over or the foundations shaken. They will, I hope, be profoundly unhappy with this book. Not that we want to stir up conflict or to argue for the sake of argument. Certainly we shall not be capable of coming to a completely satisfying definition. But only if some planks and stones are turned and some foundations are shaken can we discover what it is that we really believe about life. Perhaps those who resist the discussion are insecure about what they will find out about themselves if they think seriously. Or they are afraid of what others will think about them. In either case, if they are challenged to explain religion they will find out something fascinating: it is most difficult to stand at the edges of the argument. Like a magnet, it pulls to the center; like a whirlpool, it attracts away from the edges.

An antireligious person will profess distaste for the subject. Yet few are as engrossed by religion as are professed atheists. When they are drawn into the discussion they usually become quite vocal. People who seem most casual about religion soon lose their cool disinterest. They become personally involved. Many of them find that they have more religion in them than they had thought, and find that they cannot well describe religion except from within. The Negro musician who told the scholars that they could not intelligently discuss jazz unless they could play it would understand this. Most of the people we know claim to be somehow related to religion. If they are drawn into this most important subject, they and we can profit from exchange. We shall have much to learn.

The place of religion in the life of man

"Religion-in-general" is a name given to an American attitude and a loose system of beliefs. It points to the fact that complex societies, even those with religious freedom and thus with many religions present, tend to develop a single set of beliefs by which the nation lives. Some argue that such a development is not necessary. They say that a new kind of man and a new kind of society present themselves. In these it is possible to get along without personal religion or without a common consensus about religion in society.

CAN MAN ESCAPE RELIGION?

Is man inescapably and incurably religious? An intense debate rages on this subject. Sides are chosen chiefly along the lines described in the previous chapter. A narrow definition of religion commits one to answering that man can escape or be cured or move beyond religion. A broad definition of religion commits one to answering that man is almost by his very nature destined to be religious. He may have low religion or high religion, one religion or another, but he is somehow religious.

If religion refers to man's ability to have "ultimate concern" about someone or something to which he relates, then we would say that all are religious. If we accent man's activity, sometimes the definition begins to break down. Is an idiot religious? What is an unconscious or sleeping person doing about religion? How does an infant show religious activity? Is a thoughtless and superficial person able to think about religion?

THE ATHEIST

So widespread and attractive is American religion-in-general that very few of us know anyone who considers himself to be an atheist and who will answer for his views. Students of religion-in-general find one of the strongest points in their description to grow out of the fact that when poll-takers ask Americans about their beliefs, only about 1 per cent assert that they positively do not believe in God.

For the past century there have been people who assert that God is dead or that He never lived. He is absent or silent. He does not and cannot exist. People made this assertion for various reasons. To some the witness to God seemed to enslave man. The stench of the corpse of a dead God kept people from action. Someone had to open the windows and let in fresh air so that men might act. Atheists do this. But some say that atheists are actually the most religious, the most ultimately concerned of all. They have decided that the universe makes no sense, or makes sense apart from God. They are quite militant about their belief, and they go in pursuit of the enslaved people who believe otherwise. Clearly, one can be religious about atheism or pursue atheism religiously. He should not be "converted by definition" to an orthodox faith. It does him and the faith of his friends no good if they try to convince him that he is more or less baptized into their club because he is so concerned and impassioned. Atheism on the one hand suggests that man can escape or be cured of religion. Viewed from another angle we see that it has religious aspects.

THE AGNOSTIC

Much more common than the men who know that there is no God are those who do not know whether there is a God. The word for them was coined in the previous century. An "agnostic" says he does not know. The returns are not all in. The kinds of evidence in spiritual matters that he usually reads do not convince him. He reserves judgment. He may be impassioned in his claim that God and religion clutter up the laboratory or the legislature: that men are tempted to fall back on what they call God to bail them out of problems; that they are tempted to misuse religion to get the answers to their problems. On the other hand, he may be quite calm, cool and collected. He may mind his own business and may keep an open mind. He believes that he can affirm meaning as well without religion as with it.

Once again, the person who uses a broad definition of religion will call the agnostic a model religionist. He is supposed to be critical, and he may be reverent. He is testing the prophets and trying them, but he is not demolishing all the beliefs of others. A culture in which religion-in-general is strong is more tolerant of agnosticism, but most people in such a culture have genuine difficulty in understanding the agnostic. Religion-in-general wants to include everyone. Since the agnostic does not always resist, he is often included.

THE APATHETIC

To be apathetic means to greet the really important things of life with a shrug of the shoulders, to "play it cool" or to say, "count me out." Few young people, except those who want to get attention, make a production of being atheists. Not too many more, except for some who are quite willing to enter our serious discussion or other discussions like it, make a production of being agnostics. But many, many more are apathetic, which involves making a production out of not making a production. Great numbers of young people in particular do not want to make up their minds or be committed about something like religion.

The impulses to apathy are complex, but some of them can be understood. Young adults resent the confidence and even the bravado with which their seniors like to claim for themselves all truth in religion. These maturing people have read the history of religious wars, and they have observed pride. They dislike competitive claims for truth, so they turn their back on competitors. But most of all they are preoccupied. They are looking elsewhere: at a world which is exciting but full of problems, at a world where religion seems remote and everything else is nearer, more tangible, more exciting.

The apathetic person neither strongly disbelieves nor strongly believes in God. He is a good candidate for membership in the gatherings of religion-in-general. In his world nothing much ever happens. He has difficulty in being ultimately concerned about anything. We might call him mundane: he loses God and religious concerns in the day-to-day problems and possibilities of living.

To those who use broad definitions of religion, the apathetic are religious and they further prove that man cannot escape or be cured of religion. For the apathetic person seems, at least, to be uninterested in images and idols. Even his apparent disinterest may mask profound stirrings for God. To those who use narrow definitions of religion, the apathetic are its greatest enemies. They prove that one can cancel out religion or jam the signals it would broadcast. And if religion is escapable and if man is not incurably religious by definition, religion will be in trouble in a world where the mundane is so overpowering.

IT IS HARD TO BE NONRELIGIOUS

We conclude that man can be nonreligious if we use a narrow definition of religion. At the same time, historically, we can observe that it is notoriously difficult to sustain nonreligion and that most people at most times have been somehow religious. This fact of human practice makes matters quite easy for the proponents of religion-in-general, as we shall see.

The religious thinker observes how difficult it is for man to be permanently nonreligious. Everyone who thinks has doubts about himself, about the universe, about God. Many can go through long periods of doubt or of thoughtlessness. But as a systematic way of life nonreligion in persons has been rare, and in societies has been most rare. It is often pointed out that when Karl Marx or Nicolai Lenin asserted that God was dead, they killed religion. Yet almost every student of today's Communism sees that Communists pursue their view of history with a sense of salvation; they have messiahs; they demand ultimate sacrifice. They have not really become nonreligious by the broad definition. They have merely switched allegiances. Somehow when one religion goes, another seems to fill the vacuum. Men do not seem able to escape. They rush from the jaws of one power to the jaws of another.

HAS MAN MOVED "BEYOND RELIGION"?

Some provocative thinkers argue that man today at last is able to begin to escape. According to this argument, religion is dying and man is becoming free. Fewer people believe in astrology. They do not think the stars determine the course of man. Science is supposed to free man from many superstitions. Explanation covers for what religion used to do. God does not seem to be "out there" beyond the stars. Each year the laboratory tells me more about life than does the church. I count on science and invention to make promises and make good on them. I shall soon be free, having escaped the gods, to live on the broad plain of human freedom. If such an escape is really possible, religion-in-general will be in trouble.

In the meantime, it is not difficult to show that the old religions and the new more general ones are growing in strength. These statements at least seem to be defensible: The vast majority of men in the long record of human memory have wanted to be religious and still do. By common definitions of religion, they have succeeded and they still succeed. When they "escape" or are "cured," their new life again takes on many of the aspects of religion.

RELIGION IN MAN'S NATURE AND IN HIS PAST

If religion-in-general takes root and grows in the soil of man's natural religiousness and if religion fills his past, we can understand today's reality by recalling some of what is in man and what surrounds him.

It seems that wherever man is, he needs somehow to express belief. He has to come to terms with the thunder and lightning, the sunrise and sunset. He has to explain friendly fires and deadly animals. He lives among others and must find some basis outside the group for the life of the group. He believes that there is a power or person or purpose which relates to him. The statues of the Buddha and the shrines of Hinduism; the chants of the Muslim and the candles of the Catholic: all these witness to man's expressions of belief.

While it is not possible to argue with surety about the beliefs of people outside recorded history, we can observe that almost all traces of early life suggest some of the tools and trappings of religious response. The graves of Egyptian kings in the pyramids reveal that American undertakers did not invent the cult or religion of the dead. The statues of Roman emperors show us that a cozy alliance between God and the state was not first professed by politicians in the United States and Canada. If most of the historic religions grew out of the Mediterranean bowl or the ancient East, archeologists are able to show that American Indians, particularly in Mexico, also believed in some religious free enterprise.

RELIGION IS SUBJECT TO CHANGE

These religions were passed down from generation to generation. Sometimes they experienced subtle changes and sometimes dramatic ones. So with religion in America. In some ways it is codified in books like the Bible and in the tradition of the Church. Insofar as people follow the codes, change comes subtly. But the American environment produced startling change too. The best illustration: here first, after about seventeen hundred years, the whole society made Christianity a voluntary aspect of national life. Christianity was on its own, to persuade and argue for a place.

WHAT IS ANY RELIGION SUPPOSED TO DO FOR PEOPLE?

From the beginning, most religions have tried to represent the deity. The adherents of Islam were prevented from doing so; they merely decorated the words with which they wrote the name of God, "Allah." Before them, the ancient Jews were permitted no graven images. But these were the exception. The first thing each of us is taught about "false" religions is that their worshipers bow down to images and idols. Such learning serves to delude us or decoy us from our own problem: we fail to see how in American religion-in-general there are images too. The dollar sign or the flag will serve for many. Is there less devotion to these than there was to other idols in the past? Is man escaping religion?

Through the ages men have found or built sanctuaries for their worship and images. The beautiful tracings of animals on cave walls in France are almost certainly related to religious attitudes about nature and the hunt. The ancient Israelites carried with them in their wanderings a tent or tabernacle. Settled-down religion of Greece and Rome was housed in temples or shrines. Christians in our culture learned from all these precedents. Adherents of the general religion in our culture somehow find caves, tents or shrines for their adoration. Tour the battlefields, visit the tombs, explore the monuments, listen to the guides, and you will hear superhuman virtues and moments extolled as part of a national religion.

Religions have always been concerned with daily life. Religious founders and leaders are not content with man only visiting the scene of the shrine. People are to infuse all of life with their religious vision. Meals, candles, books in the home, sacred pictures: these have helped bridge the

world of the shrine and the world of the market. They still
do. A sacred meal of bread and wine once served to bring
people to their greatest moments of joy and fellowship.
Today a banquet or a cocktail party still offers such eu-
charist and fellowship. People regard these latter events
with a great sense of ritual and religious regard.

Religions concern themselves with all the chief moments
of life. Birth, initiation, maturing, marriage, death: each of
these produce religious occasions and are related to religion. It is interesting to observe that when a totalitarian
power wants to abolish historic faiths, it has to and wants
to provide parallels for these sacred events. Both the Nazis
before World War II and the Communists since have had
state ceremonies by which the child is received into society,
in which adults are married, in which the dead are honored.
A Dutch churchman says that in culture-religion (including
its Christian forms) people come to the shrine only on four
wheels: baby-buggies, marriage limousines, or hearses, to
be hatched, matched, and dispatched. In American culture-
religion great attention is paid to these rites.

PAGANISM IN CHRISTIAN SOCIETY

Sometimes the rites are historically Christian but are
taken over by the society. Often the most relaxed church
affiliates give most attention to the detail of a baptism: the
child's dress, the time of the day, the vintage of champagne
for a baptismal dinner. While marriages even in Christian
society have never been wholly purged of their pagan details, today more than ever the religion of culture uses the
church for weddings. As is well known, the poor clergyman
in such circumstances has little control over the music, the
customs and the ceremonies. He may try to sneak in a few
words about God. But the people in church are in real con-

trol: the wedding involves a use of the sacred building and memory for the glorification of two humans, two families. And many people who have not seen the inside of a church or been in the presence of a clergyman for many years still are brought to it or to him feet first for burial.

As people more and more turn to the mundane, they seem more and more to need the religious type of ceremonies to fill the void in times of crisis. A veterans' organization or a fraternal lodge can produce the most religious-looking ceremony at the time of death. A college fraternity, having in mind only the most vague and nebulous picture of God, can contrive the most elaborate religious-sounding rituals for initiation. Man does not easily escape religion in the most important moments of life.

EDUCATION AND CREEDS

The religions of man have ordinarily had considerable interest in educating their adherents. How otherwise will these pass the faith on through time? Especially when education was by word of mouth, before the majority of people could read and write, such education was disciplined in religious groups. A religion produced by a culture may not have a formal program of education. It hardly needs one. The whole culture gets its signals across. For instance, in so far as patriotism or Americanism is a part (and it is only a part) of religion-in-general, it hardly needs a program of education. The public schools, the mass media of communication, the politicians, the home: each of these serve as instruments to support the more or less religious devotion given to national symbols. When these symbols are threatened, as in the case of the assault by what is called atheistic Communism, some people begin to feel the need of a formal program. Soon textbooks and codebooks appear. An American creed begins to develop. Conformity is enforced. Opinions are channeled to serve the patriotic religion's need.

The very nature of generalized religion defies putting it down in neat categories or doctrines. If you were forced to pick out general features of the general God of general religion, you might end up with these:

He is understandable and manageable, and has been generalized and redesigned for mass consumption.

He is comforting, so that "believing" comes to mean having the "proper connection with the higher powers."

He is one of us, an American... or Canadian or British... a jolly good fellow whose "gospel" makes us "feel real good." [1]

I repeat, precise definition is difficult. But the end product is unquestionably a comfortable familiarity, a God-on-our-terms, and a divine-human chumminess, a God-on-our-side.

When religions educate and as they develop creeds and orthodoxies (systems of right belief), they try to relate to all of life. We chose nationalism as a part of the religion of our culture. We could reach in many directions. Whenever we use the word "Credo" or creed we refer to something which is somehow believed in religiously. In 1962 Stuart Chase wrote a book, *American Credos*. In it he analyzed the belief-systems to which Americans hold with great seriousness and even with ultimate concern. After telling the story of how poll-taking and interviewing about opinion has become a full-time science, he gives an organized account of the creeds of Americans.

Admittedly, not every one would find himself in Chase's portrait. Not every one considers his own random and hap-

[1] See pp. 37-39 in *The New Shape of American Religion*, by Martin E. Marty, New York: Harper & Brothers, 1959.

hazard belief-systems gathered from daily life as seriously as he regards historic religion. But Chase and countless other analysts argue in the opposite direction: the regard we show for historic religion has to be related to the basic choices we make in other areas of life.

Thus Chase has a chapter on American "creeds" that have to do with belief in One World or in Our Nation and its foreign policy; there is a well-known American Business Creed, and author Chase even includes one chapter that treats of the public's ideas about "Work" as a creed, as articles of faith. There are creeds in the realms of Politics, Education, Science, Civil Liberties, and Personal Problems. In a 216-page book, exactly four pages are devoted to "Attitudes toward Religion."

Chase quotes C. Lloyd Warner: "All societies adjust their members to the unknown—those forces which technology cannot explain or control sufficiently to offer the individual safety. Religion and magic with myth and ritual are the accredited methods for accomplishing this fearful task." Chase shows how most Americans consider themselves to be devout Christians or Jews. But the surveys show that surface appearances are deceptive. Chase cites a survey which revealed that 73 per cent of the American people believed in life after death, with God as Supreme Judge. Only 5 per cent, however, expressed any fear of hell. By this reference he wants to show that we are incurably and inescapably religious. But we feel free to improvise with the religions we profess and to take the seriousness and the sting out of them. Concludes Chase: "The old faiths are losing their grip, but the 'fearful task' of adjusting members of a society to the unknown is more challenging than ever."

I do not want to suggest that Chase's survey is the last

2 *American Credos,* New York: Harper & Brothers, 1962, pp. 182-85.

word or that he has located historic faith properly in all respects. But he and his countless colleagues are telling us something quite important about ourselves: we are capable of producing the creeds and propagating them. And these new creeds tend to overpower the old ones which we like to keep around and by which we want to be measured.

SEEING RELIGION IN OTHERS

Wilfred Cantwell Smith has pointed out that "religion" is a rather stuffy, tired and static word. When people begin to waver in their faith in Christ they start talking about Christianity. When they grow uncertain about Christianity they take their defense in religion-in-general. But the most vital Christians do not like to have their faith called a religion. Argues Smith: neither do adherents of other faiths. Those who really know, know that religion when it has grown stuffy, tired and static, is a kind of "dirty" word. It takes the place of living faith in a living God.

We can see this best if we look at the religions produced in the culture of people with whom we do not agree. Jules Monnerot, in *Sociology and Psychology of Communism,* takes the instance of Communism in a passage which will reveal something to us about religion:

> To an educated European or American, unless he is himself a communist, it appears that communists are religious fanatics. . . But communists see it differently: for them communism is *what ought to be,* and the whole of history, the whole past of humanity, takes its meaning from this future event.

> Communism is on its way. A religion is seen as such only by those outside it. For its adherents it is simply the highest form of truth. For the true believer Russia no longer exists as such; but he does not believe he is

a believer; he believes he possesses the truth. In fact, he is *possessed* by something which he believes to be the truth; and for this truth he feels an active attachment of a kind which truth (at least scientific truth) does not usually inspire or demand.[3]

In passing, let us note that when Monnerot wants to make a comparison he calls Communism "The Twentieth-Century Islam." In his mind Christianity is not sufficiently creedal or militant or possessed to deserve comparison.

Now, the educated European or American will have the Russian's problem in reverse. He will not see how a capitalist free economic system can become a religion in the eyes of others. (Russia, for instance, is much more worried about our religion of business or of science than about our attachments to historic Christianity.) To the educated American his system is *"what ought to be,* and the whole of history, the whole past of humanity, takes its meaning from this future event." His system is seen as a religion only by those outside it. For our adherents "it is simply the highest form of truth." We are possessed by what we believe to be the truth, while they see us to be devoted to a religion which they can dismiss.

WHO BELIEVES IN RELIGION-IN-GENERAL?

While we are on this point, an important parenthesis is in order. I am not under any illusions, and no reader who agrees with the general plot of this book should be under any either: most people described as adherents of our culture's specific religion-in-general would not recognize themselves in every detail out of the whole. Many of them would resent having their belief-system called a religion. From six to nine out of ten would call themselves Christians or ad-

[3] Boston: Beacon Press, 1953, p. 20.

herents of the Judeo-Christian religion, whatever that is. Their belief system appears to them to be nothing more than that; but to those outside it, it is a religion. (I am also not so fatuous as to suggest that you readers and I stand wholly outside it. We cannot and do not want to escape our culture. Inevitably we find ourselves assenting to elements of religion-in-general. We do not even recognize them. Only those who disagree with us will. I shall also try to suggest some potentially redemptive features in American religion. Not all its detail is bad; the thing itself is what produces the trouble.)

WHERE SHALL WE STAND?

If we want to stand partly outside this apparently casual belief system and make meaningful comment, we shall have to determine where we stand in the great outside. There must be some place for viewing and some sort of measure or norm. We are going to try to see religion-in-general from the viewpoint of historic Christianity as witnessed to in the Bible and in the creedal tradition of Christianity. Those who are seen to hold to religion-in-general but who want to be judged by Christianity will then have one or another of these obligations: (1) To show that our definitions of "religion" are mistaken or misleading; (2) or to show that the substance or content of "religion-in-general" has been inaccurately described and does not apply; (3) or to show that our description of Christian faith is inaccurate or misleading; (4) or to show that religion-in-general and historic Christianity are compatible; (5) or to show that historic Christianity can be legitimately transformed and changed into something that can agree with or complement religion-in-general.

There may be other options, but these at least are present. This should be made clear: in this book no attempt will be made philosophically to prove that Christianity is the true religion and that religion-in-general is false. My argument would be wholly unconvincing to a Muslim, who might well be able from his viewpoint to show the superiority of religion-in-general. I can not try here to do any more than this: to say to people who want their beliefs and their culture to be measured by historic Christianity, "How do your actual and professed belief system and way of life measure up to the yardstick which you have agreed should serve as the measure?"

WHAT IS THE FUTURE OF RELIGION?

Throughout this chapter the clear implication has been given that religion appeals to something deep in the nature of man. More confidently it has been said that most people are somehow religious and that as they escape or are cured of one religion they come into the orbit or power of another. The historian cannot prophesy or predict or project. So I cannot say, "Will man some day escape and be cured?" Psychologists who study the nature of man and theologians who comment on the nature of God have to engage in that kind of talk. But since the answers they give have some bearing on our description of religion-in-general it is necessary, at least, to provide a minority report from theological circles. Perhaps the most provocative of these talkers-about-God was the late Dietrich Bonhoeffer, who in 1945 was killed in a Nazi concentration camp. Bonhoeffer foresaw and his disciples and others recognize that across the world something new is appearing. People are coming past the religious stage of world history. Religion with its explanations belonged to the infancy or the adolescence of man and the world. But now the world has come of age, or at least it is coming of age.

According to this interpretation, each year more and more people will not look beyond this world for meaning or explanation. They will, for the first time at least in our culture, feel reasonably at home in a universe without God. They do not experience Him "out there" looking in on man and they do not find Him "in here" when they search their laboratories or their hearts. Each year they cause religious people to retreat a bit further.

THE RELIGIOUS RETREAT

Centuries ago, we are told, Christians fought off the early scientists who wanted to assert that the earth was not the center of creation. After violent disagreements with Galileo and Copernicus, Christians retreated and "joined" those whom they had not "licked." God no longer was just beyond the rim of the heavens. But He was still out there, a bit further. Each time there was a new telescope or a new discovery He got pushed further back, until people lost faith that He was out there at all. Each year as scientists make new discoveries religious people say that God is a bit further out there, where human ignorance comes in. But when man finds explanation he ceases to need God.

This is admittedly an oversimplified story and it verges on caricature. Christians were not all that blind and stupid, either in the way they observed or the way they argued. But many of them have acted this way enough to give people around them the clear impression that the God who was hiding behind the curtains of man's probing where man's ignorance begins is not there at all. If we follow Bonhoeffer's projection, the day is coming when man can leave behind not only historic faiths but his religious nature itself. Religion would go the way of superstition. (Christian thinker Bonhoeffer seemed to believe that this process would in no way threaten faith in Jesus Christ and would, in fact, liberate Christians and bring them to adulthood. How he argued that is another story which cannot be detailed here.)

If man can really be devoted to the world as a thing rounded off in itself, religion-in-general will look different. It will not need symbols like the word "God" which appears so frequently in it now. Man may really become the liberated and happy agnostic, and may become the ally of the Christian against religion-in-general and other human productions. The historian is interested in these possibilities, but he cannot join the theologian in such confident statements about man's nature and dare not join him in such daring pictures of the future. He can only say what he sees has developed in other societies and in his own.

Some people seem to belong to a "world come of age." Some of them seem to be able to move out of historic faiths and then to succeed in doing something much more difficult: to be *really agnostic* and to withhold their loyalties from the obvious features of religion-in-general. But in general man's "escape from religion" has not become successful or complete. Sometimes people appear to have escaped only to fall back into magic and superstition. Or they devise new and different means of expressing themselves religiously.

SIDE BY SIDE

For the moment, what can we do? We can observe that most people of the world are committed to one or another of the world's formal religions. We can proceed further and say that most of the world's uncommitted people live in cultures which are somehow defined by a religious remembrance. Third, the general trend of the past century has been both toward the revival of the historic faiths and to the development of new ones. We can also see that all the religions are threatened by nonreligion and by a picture of the universe which is wholly accidental, meaningless, and absurd. In our culture we are contending that most adherents of historic faith live side by side with a generalized religion which has borrowed from their history and to which they now are supplying converts or sharing believers.

What's in a name?
Religion-in-general
and Christianity

One sunny morning a discontented man awoke. He took a deep breath and thought to himself, "I do not like the existing religions around me. I think I will start a new one." So he left his little hut in the hills and went to the big city. He became a prophet and a preacher. Soon he had a following. He and his followers attacked the existing religions, as he had said he himself would. Eventually the new faith began to take on an outline. More and more people identified with it. They built shrines and devised codes and creeds. Finally they held a great council and decided to name their new faith "American religion-in-general."

Of course, that is *not* how religion-in-general got started. By telling it in that silly way it is possible for me to make clear something or other about its origin or purpose. Up to this point we have been comparing it to the formal or "high" religions of the world. It seems absurd to take an informal religious complex almost accidentally put together and set it seriously alongside Buddhism, Hinduism, Islam, Judaism, or Christianity. But all of the great religions include many accidental features. All of them worked like vacuum cleaners, picking up something or other from their environments. All of them worked like blowers, pushing

48

away other elements from the worlds which surrounded them.

The religions which command the attention of hundreds of millions of people, however, did tend to have more clearly identifiable beginnings. In most cases there was a prophet, someone dissatisfied with existing religions. He would feel called by God to bring in a new age or to lead people to a new place. He would storm against existing religions and attract disciples to something new. He would carefully select features of the world around him with which to make an appeal to would-be followers. He would carefully resist the suffocating embrace of those who would absorb his spiritual energies into existing religions. He and his followers would soon give their movement a name or, more likely, would have to settle for one given them by strangers or enemies.

In dealing with American religion-in-general we are at a loss to point to such identifiable movements and leaders. There is no founder, no clear-cut argument with existing religion, no attempt to make up codes or creeds, no desire to manufacture a name. In a quiet way it is missionary and it certainly attracts followers, though few if any of them would be conscious of joining a movement or a club. Few would recognize that they are being called to give up anything in their religious past. There is no universally agreed-upon name by which their faith is called.

WHAT'S IN A NAME?

In this book we have settled for "religion-in-general," with hyphens and all. Any number of other terms might have done as well. We could call it America's culture-religion. It has been shaped by the experience of the North American nations and particularly by the United States.

It could not be understood apart from the needs of Americans. By calling it a culture-religion we would be pointing to one feature: that nothing in it serves to criticize or judge the generally agreed-upon values of the whole society.

Another name might be Americanism. But this is misleading too. Like most "isms," Americanism attracts people with all the seriousness that historic faiths used to have. A person can treat Americanism as an instrument by which to express his highest values and his ultimate concern. He is more likely to be called to give his life for it than for Christianity, and is more likely to respond. It is easier for him to be spotted as a heretic or traitor to that faith than to be regarded as a deviator from Christianity or some other historic religion. But Americanism conjures up only one feature of this cultural creed, its nationalist feature. What name can be used to describe other aspects of our culture-religion?

Try again: it could be the Religion of the American Way of Life. This is much more accurate, but also much more cumbersome. It is more accurate because it does serve to justify a whole Way: nationhood, business, success, personal life, material prosperity and other matters can all be absorbed into it. Some might choose the term "religiosity" to cover the whole field. Religiosity refers to man in the act of being religious without reference to what his object of belief may be.

THE NAME IS A HANDLE

"Generalized religion" or "religion-in-general" has been chosen by any number of students of American life in the past two decades. It is a term that seems to impose itself logically on our minds. The chief features are implied in the term itself: it is general as opposed to particular. That is, it would rather absorb than fight off other religions or idea-systems in the American environment. It is a religion, so it cannot be dismissed as a merely random and momentary element of national life. I have no interest in advertising or contending for the term; if a better one comes along we should use it. Religion-in-general is, then, a mere tool or handle for trying to hold something which would slip away entirely if we made no attempt to define or confine it at all.[1]

It goes without saying (so we had better say it) that one of the most distinctive features of American religion-in-general is that it *remembers* the main religious tradition of America, namely the Judeo-Christian. Its Bible is the Old and New Testament of the Scriptures, though it may crowd this book with other documents. Almost nothing in it, naturally, is consciously derived from Islam or Buddhism. Parallels between it and other religions there are, but they are largely accidental.

Hinduism and American religion-in-general both satisfy a need in many people to try to overcome religious conflict by minimizing religious differences. Islam and American religion-in-general are both militant against the complete outsider. This feature may seem to contradict the other one; actually it applies to different aspects of need. Hindu-

---

[1] "What is the explanation of the situation which exists in the United States? The situation has been described in various ways by the analysts of our society. Roy Eckardt uses the term 'folk religion'; Martin Marty's phrase is 'religion-in-general'; and Will Herberg contends that the real religion of Americans is 'The American Way of Life' . . . Franklin Littell prefers the phrase 'culture-religion' . . . All of these descriptions point to the same conclusion: the Gospel is identified with 'democracy' and capitalism; religion is *used* to defend and to support individual and national goals . . . In the United States the churches must combat the tendency to identify the Gospel with the American way of life."—Kenneth Cauthen in the *Bulletin of Crozer Theological Seminary*, July, 1964.

ism helps people live with their neighbors and Islam helps hold people together with a sense of destiny by pushing back the outsider. American religion-in-general helps most Americans live with each other, but in order to hold them together it needs and builds up all kinds of foreign devils (such as atheistic Communism) as foils or contrasts.

FEEDING ON CHRISTIANITY

It is on Christianity, with elements of Judaism, that American religion-in-general directly feeds. The developing culture-religion is not sectarian, but it remembers Protestantism best of all. The reasons for this are clear. Judaism was hardly represented at all in the thirteen colonies from the early seventeenth century to the late eighteenth. Even Roman Catholicism probably had only about 20,000 people in a population of four and a half million people when the nation was born. While Roman Catholics were soon to come by the millions, so that they had become the largest single religious group in the United States well over a century ago, they were guests in a host culture. Sometimes welcome and sometimes not, they were strangers in the power centers of the nation. Protestants in effect ran the show. The majority of the people were not church members until well into the twentieth century. But the majority of the people traded on the strength of Protestantism.

Ask an American who is not Jewish or Roman Catholic what he is religiously and he will usually say "Protestant," unless he uses the name of a Protestant denomination. In about half of the instances no Protestant minister or congregation knows he is Protestant, and he may attend church nowhere. But to be non-Jewish or non-Catholic, except for about 3 per cent of the population which calls itself "uncommitted" or "other," means to consider oneself in the Protestant tradition.

That seems to leave almost no one around who could join a religion-in-general club. It seems to leave almost no one to argue with the basic tenets of Judaism, Catholicism, or Protestantism. Yet whenever surveys are taken, the people who analyze them find that the majority of the American people indeed do not know or, if they find out, disagree with those basic tenets of Judaism, Catholicism and Protestantism which contradict basic tenets of religion-in-general.

We are allowing for the possibility in theory that people can escape the historic religions of America, and we can observe that a few people say they do. At the same time we shall suggest that most people who are inactive in the churches and many who are active, if they escape the historic religions, find a home in a newer religion which reminds them of what they liked and what did not disturb them in the old.

IN THE COURSE OF A LIFE

One of the best ways to see a person joining the religion-in-general cluster is to see what happens to a typical child as he matures.

To the tiny child there is only one religion. It is inherited. He does not ordinarily come into contact with any outside his family circle and, if he did, would not often be able to appraise or choose between religions. His response is derived from his parents, nurses, or earliest teachers. He inhabits a cozy universe of meaning. When he prays before meals he will say "Come, Lord Jesus," and not a Buddhist prayer. He will adopt a facsimile of his parents' postures.

As time passes this little universe breaks up. He catches father telling a lie or finds his parents fighting. How much can he trust their teaching? They withdraw so that he can mature. He feels cheated and insecure. He reaches out to friends and becomes acquainted with their views.

By the time of adolescence he is "properly shook up." He lives in a Christian culture. Christians tell him, "Love thy neighbor" and work for concord with all. But he finds that in his town Methodist, Lutheran, Baptist and Catholic Christians are competing for their slice of the pie, and their actions tell him, "Shove thy neighbor." Which will he believe? Meanwhile he meets people of other faiths at school. He learns of other cultures and religions. He experiences what social thinkers call "identity diffusion:" he does not know who is or what he believes or where he fits in.

In college, in military service, at the beginning of his career he is more or less on his own. He may reject some of his childhood outlook, including religion. He takes a job and moves around in a society which constantly places him where he must get along with people who believe differently than he does. He sees the need for national unity and good relations with others. He rejoins the church, but he is sure that he wants nothing to do with divisive religion. Who can blame him? So he agrees with those who tell him that all religions are the same, but that everyone ought to have one. And he agrees with those who say that the only one who should be ruled out of his belief-system is the complete outsider like the Communist or the foreigner. Within the narrower context, at least as long as nothing is troubling him, he will keep on being tolerant and loving everybody and certainly not arguing religion.

He may go to church, but he gets his basic signals for life from outside it. Insofar as these signals are religious, he will prefer receiving them over radio or television, from celebrity preachers who have reworked the Christian gospel so that it will appeal to him. He will follow Christianity and the church up to a certain point. The moment he is asked to give up any basic feature of the world view he put together outside of church, he makes his choice for the culture-religion. He is a member of a Christian church, not a member of a religion-in-general club. (There are none.) He is a Christian and not, he says, a believer in religion-in-general. We want to believe him, but we shall put him to the test.

WHAT IS A CHRISTIAN?

I will not presume to be the man who answers the question which has troubled the Christian world for a thousand years. It would be silly to try to spell out in detail all features of Christianity on which all can and should agree. The obvious divisions of Christianity despite good efforts to bring about reunion should lead us to mistrust anyone who has a do-it-yourself religious unity kit he wants to offer us.

On the other hand, Christian disunity is not so chaotic that we cannot see how Christians despite differences have more in common with each other than they do with the world religions or with the culture-religions which surround them. Let us restrict ourselves to two features. For shorthand reasons I will take my statement indirectly from the greatest systematic thinker Christianity has known, St. Thomas Aquinas.

According to the theologians, the essence of the Christian faith can be summed up in two words. Those two words are Trinity and Incarnation. The "universal teacher" of Christendom has said that the whole content of the truth of Christian faith can be reduced to the dogma of the Trinitarian God and the dogma that man participates in the life of God through Christ.[2]

[2] These words, including the paraphrase of Aquinas' Latin definition —which we will not permit to trouble us here—are by Josef Pieper, *Belief and Faith,* New York: Pantheon Books, 1963, p. 103.

Christians have many other beliefs which grow out of and are based on these two. Nothing Christians teach is to be in contradiction to these two. There are many additional details. There may be small quibbles. Not all Christians use the word "Trinity," and some deviate slightly from the full meaning of that to which it refers. Not all find a Latin word like "Incarnation" meaningful and not all accept its full implications.

The Roman Catholic half of the Christian world certainly agrees in the main with Aquinas' summary. The Orthodox millions would also agree. Protestants in the World Council of Churches have as a basis of their witness a sentence which implies these two themes. Conservative Protestants who have nothing to do with the World Council do not disagree with these central expressions.

The first, Trinity, refers to a God who has revealed himself as Father, Son and Holy Spirit. Symbolically it means that God exists outside the realm of my experience, He "transcends" my world, and takes the initiative to address me. The second, Incarnation, also refers to the fact that this transcending God from outside my world enters it and addresses me. He does so particularly and uniquely in Jesus Christ, who is incarnate or takes on my condition as a human being.

To be a Christian begins with belief in at least these two dimensions of Christian witness. It implies some assent to Christian purpose. It defines me over against those who do not witness to the Father, Son, and Holy Spirit who transcend my world. It defines me over against those who disbelieve in Jesus Christ or who find His place in my world to be accidental, arbitrary, or unnecessary.

We do not deny that the setting in which these teachings appear changes from age to age and place to place. We are not pretending that this definition will settle arguments of emphasis or detail. But we need not bend over backward in shyness because we cannot say everything. Stated negatively, Christians do not *not*-believe in the Trinity (as Buddhists, Shintoists, Jews do not-believe) and they do not *not*-believe in the Incarnation (as Hindus, Muslims, and other world religionists do not-believe).

WHO ELSE BELIEVES THIS?

What about general religionists? In America most of them would begin with some assent to these central teachings. The crucial difference comes in when they assert, quietly but clearly, that whatever else may be true it is not absolutely necessary to begin here in religion. More important, these teachings do not matter too much. Most important, if one does not happen to believe these, but if he does have a belief, all will be well with him.

We are now at the point of "the great divide." We do not need to enter into the questions of just how noisy and obnoxious Christians feel they have to become in separating themselves from other kinds of believers. We do not have to argue with those who insist on putting a much finer point on Christian doctrines and teachings. We are only saying provisionally that if this is what Christianity is at its base, it should be the measure of the basic teachings of a culture-religion that has hitchhiked and become a fellow-traveler.

The general religionist may argue, I want to redefine Christianity. I want to think of it as a way of life, a general philosophy or pattern or set of principles. How can he camp on his definition? To him we have to say as historians, look at the record. Of course one can call anything whatever he wants. I can call Communism "the twentieth-century Islam" but I will make no sense to my audience if I try to argue that Communism and Islam today represent the same thing in detail. I may draw a long-legged, long-necked yellow and brown animal and called it a rhinoceros. But it will keep on being a giraffe to those who want to be careful with words and things. That God *is* Father, Son, and Spirit and that He *acts* in Jesus Christ, seem to be integral to the Christian statement. That Christians in their Scriptures have no consistent and clear revelation about God's plan outside Trinity and Incarnation is also clearer than the general religionist wants to let it be. (There are a few clues, and we will look at them after a while.)

The motive behind defining the difference is a desire for clarity only. We have no interest in "filling up hell" as some of our less lovable church fathers did. They advertised the delights of heaven as consisting partly in the vision the saints in glory would have as they peep over the rim of heaven at all their old rakish buddies now suffering below. Christianity resists the embrace of culture-religion not for the sake of being uncharitable or superior but for the sake of clarity and service.

People can basically and consciously repudiate the center of the Christian faith. In our culture they are not likely to do this on a widespread scale. More likely they will unconsciously surround the faith with other teachings which will crowd out its distinctiveness. This is the point of the birth of religion-in-general.

HOW DOES RELIGION-IN-GENERAL DEVELOP?

Americans, as we shall see later, are surprisingly orthodox in their Christian faith. Most of them on the surface at least hold to its central teachings. We say "surprisingly" because in a free society we would expect people to express themselves at great variance from the ways in which the established and more popular religions express themselves. It is surprising because in a scientific world we would think they would be immediately troubled by the radical and miraculous Christian teachings. But on the surface, before we examine religion-in-general, all seems secure, serene, and unchanging.

What is happening? Most observers of the religious scene agree with a sociologist like Professor J. Milton Yinger. He too ponders: why do not Americans deviate more than they seem to from the historic faiths? Why do they not join religion-in-general clubs? Yinger finds that in America as in many other complex cultures there are "persons acting religiously in a way that does not express directly the faith they profess." They redefine their religion "while disguising or obscuring the process by holding, somewhat superficially, to many of the symbols of the earlier religious system."

What we are witnessing is the development of new religious forms. The life conditions of the middle and upper classes in our urban societies, so dramatically different from anything mankind has ever before experienced, are having significant religious consequences. The changes are being obscured by the continuity of symbols; they are, quite understandably, opposed by most religious professionals—with the result that much of the new religion is developing at the hands of laymen—but the changes continue nevertheless.[3]

Yinger would probably agree with historian Franklin Baumer in calling religion-in-general a new "laymen's religion" or with Duncan Howlett in calling it "America's Fourth Faith." At any rate, something new is emerging

[3] In *Sociology Looks at Religion*, New York: The Macmillan Company, 1963, pp. 69-72 *passim*.

right under the noses of religious leaders and faithful church members. Maybe it is time for something new and better to develop; the general religionist is not likely to agree that something new is here. He wants what Yinger calls "continuity of symbols." He likes to have Trinity and Incarnation around but to surround them with new meanings.

THREE DIRECTIONS FROM WHICH THE RELIGION COMES

Religion-in-general can be derived naturally from Christianity; that is, one can "slip down" into it. Christians believe that discipleship is difficult and that their faith when strong and pure is a hard, narrow, high road. What they often call "the natural man" is naturally interested in coming down from it to a religion which he can control or in embracing a God which he can dangle like a doll. Morally he finds a controllable religion more attractive. Intellectually it is his natural faith; he does not really need to change any attitudes which are now present. So he falls into the new religious choice.

A second and opposite direction which can motivate religion-in-general is the upward climb. Some people find features of Christianity to be too easy, too tired, too lifeless. They think America needs a better religion than it has. It must make greater demands than the historic faiths can make and must offer promises greater than they promise. As Walter Lippman noticed over forty years ago, Christianity does not incarnate many human desires today. Perhaps morally and intellectually superior men can invent a religion which will better prepare people for a new day. Quaint teachings like the Trinity and the Incarnation were all right for a cozier past, but we need less comfortable and more meaningful symbols for the present. (It is my view that this is a rare version of the change, but it is present among a few articulate general religionists.)

The third direction is perhaps the most common: it is horizontal. One can slide into it sideways without recognizing what is happening. All religions which are not sectarian, which are not radically cut off from their surroundings, make this possible. They want to serve and they want to attract. They must adopt some language and practice from the surroundings; soon people cannot tell the difference. If Christianity were in no danger of sliding over into a culture-religion, it would succeed in proving to us nothing but that it is withdrawn and does not care about the world around it.

I am saying that the environment produces the need for additions to or parallels to Christianity. Having produced the need, it also produces the answers or fulfillments. And in that rich and resourceful circle, it provides the magnet or the attraction. When the frustrated and weary children of Israel in the wilderness asked for a Golden Calf to worship, Aaron satisfied them. It was made of their earrings and their jewels. It was their controllable god, their invention. He did not have to engage in advertising to attract them to it!

People are attracted to American religion-in-general because they believe in it, they share its views. It may have a few official priests and codebooks, but it hardly needs them; it naturally attracts. Some may find it professionally profitable to cater to people's general religious interest. We shall not obscure our argument here by examining such motives. When it comes to holding the loyalties of people, American "religion-in-general" is such a natural expression that we need not reach far to see how it attracts or how it is sustained. We need not read anything sinister into the lives of people who minister to its adherents.

MAKING THE TEST

A generalized culture-religion which ultimately decides against Christianity eventually will show up when the two are tested. We can take an example in the instance of race. It is often observed that the Christian witness makes its way so long as it deals with the little virtues and vices at the edges of life. When it confronts a profound and basic human emotion it is rejected.

What about religion-in-general and race? It asserts, of course, that all men in America and all their beliefs—if they are religious—are generally acceptable. Of course, these beliefs and sentiments are rather abstract. One talks about them more than he acts upon them. But one is not called to do something directly to recognize and share the lives of others, to make concrete the freedom of all men. (I do not mean that religion-in-generalists are all racially prejudiced more than are their contemporaries. I am saying that they have fewer resources for judging prejudice.)

Now, what about Christianity? It asserts that God in Jesus Christ has made men absolutely and perfectly free. He has broken down walls and barriers between men. He has created a new community of perfect human fellowship. In practice men may frustrate details of that perfection. But they may not go about basically denying the freedom and the fellowship and calling the denial Christian. In Christ God has made the Negro or the Oriental free. By identifying with our race He has honored all its members.

When a nominal Christian who moves with apparent freedom in the realms of generalized religion is confronted with the ways in which his manner of life contradicts Christian freedom and fellowship, he has his answers. When he is told that *he* is the one who is not free, that he must work with masks and illusions and false words, that he is not free really to meet or to serve the brother, he answers that he really wants it that way. His minister may say, "You'd better get right with your colored neighbor now; you will have to share heaven with him." He may, as likely as not, reply that he does not want anything to do with such a heaven. And he means it.

The Christian is to see the difference between God's purposes and those of his nation. He is to know that God who "sits in the heavens" laughs at nations which set themselves up as the controllers of history, as the all-powerful and all-knowing. But the "Christian" religion-in-general adherent says, "My country, right or wrong." He is sure that the Almighty has worked out an especially cozy relationship with his own country. He knows that there cannot be a real conflict of purpose between his god and his nation, if that nation is run as he wants it to be. Again, when a basic human attachment like nationalism is first enthroned, religion-in-general protects it so that distinctive Christianity cannot judge it.

Each of us can easily discover other illustrations out of our own hearts: is it our pursuit of success or money or reputation that needs a belief-system, that needs a god to protect it? Religion-in-general, because it is in part my product and is invented or tailored by me, serves to protect that pursuit.

Locating religion-in-general's true believers

TRACKING DOWN RELIGION-IN-GENERAL

We have made many rash and some rather unkind remarks about the development of a culture-religion which bears some resemblance to but surrounds and undercuts Christianity in America. We have shown how to account for the development of such a religious attitude and why not to be surprised by it. We have not proved its existence.

One of the best ways for each reader to make up his mind is to involve himself in thought about people's religious attitudes. He can inform himself about the historic Christian faith. Then he can interview and question people. What do they know about that faith? How does it inform their lives? At what point do they surrender it for the sake of competing views?

We need not content ourselves, however, with mere intuitions and impressions. During the past century almost every foreign observer to our shores, from Lord Bryce to André

Siegfried through Daniel W. Brogan, has remarked our peculiar religious make-up. Most historians and students of American spirituality have been impressed by the inventiveness with which we have devised and then obscured from view our new secular religion. But most of all, over the past couple of decades, social analysts have developed instruments for interviewing and poll-taking. They have applied these to religion. They have published their findings. Virtually all the findings emphatically underscore the presence of "laymen's religion" or religion-in-general.

A book of this type can be overburdened if the author hauls in too much of the impressive apparatus of an academic document. Every footnote chases away readers. I shall not do here as I often do elsewhere, document in detail the picture of religion-in-general. I shall speak in broader terms, referring to the work of a number of authors by name but leaving detailed inquiry up to those readers who want to pursue it. They can consult libraries or professionals; most ministers can guide them to the literature. They should be aware, as am I, that social analysis is not infallible. It does not tell us all about the subtleties of religion. But when many different people work with different samples of the population, using different tools and hoping to find a variety of things, and *then* find that their conclusions overwhelmingly agree, we should take note.

So I have before me as I write, books which have tested religious opinion in rural communities, small towns, suburbs, cities and inner cities in the United States and Canada. Regionally there are samples from the Midwest, the South, the Northeast and the Far West. What about age-groups? Beginning with high school, we work through college, the early years of marriage and into the family years. There are surveys in conservative and liberal denominations. Protestants, Catholics, Jews, the nonchurched are represented. Active and inactive church members are compared. Negro religion has been given separate attention. Finally, there are one or two surveys which have tried to be comprehensive; they cover any gaps. I know of no substantial differences in their general findings. Oh yes, here and there an author wants to be cantankerous or original; he may want to sell a book. But when we are finished we find his sample is also part of the pattern. What is clear in them all?

1. Americans are nominally surprisingly conventional or orthodox about their faith.

2. Over half of them know almost nothing distinctive about it.

3. Over half of them, if they are church members, have adopted a set of basic attitudes which undercut distinctive Christian beliefs.

4. Most of them have surrounded their Christian beliefs with cultural views which may or may not be compatible with Christianity, but which their holders automatically believe are compatible.

5. Insofar as it can be determined, in the daily practices of living, the teachings of religion-in-general prevail over those of specific Christianity.

The surveys that should be most interesting to young people are those which deal with young people. The study which directly occasioned this book was a four-year study of 3,000 high school youth in the Lutheran Church. Lutherans, many of you know, have a reputation for doctrinal conservatism. That is, they widely advertise their devotion to historic faith. Further, they are known for the seriousness with which they instruct people just before high school. This survey, headed by Merton P. Strommen, therefore leads us to an age level in a denominational group where religion-in-general should be about as weak as any-where in American religion.

In these surveys the young people did not seem desirous of being thought of as unfaithful to God and Church or heedless of historic Christianity. But they experienced "iden-tity diffusion." Their distinctiveness had never appeared or, where it had, was already swallowed up in general belief. I might try to summarize by saying that the more distinc-tively Christian and the more distinctively Lutheran a teach-ing was, the less it was understood or held to by the young people to whom such a distinction was to have been a definition.

Let me lay my cards on the table. In a research brief, Dr. Strommen informed me of some aspects of the life of those who he said held to the tenets of religion-in-general. While their attitudes served to dull the edge of moral alertness, this dulling did not serve to grant them real peace or real free-dom. In fact, they

> tend to be least aware of God's forgiveness and most con-fused as to what the church teaches. They are less willing than average to admit to what is uncomplimentary and more likely to express displeasure over family relation-ships. One out of four would exclude Negroes from the church fellowship and one out of two would grant mar-riage privileges to the unmarried. On the dimensions of religious commitment they score at the low end of the distribution.

What about those who reject religion-in-general?

> They tend to be aware of God's forgiveness, and show clarity in matters of Christian doctrine. They are more willing than average to admit to what is uncomplimen-tary and less likely to be troubled over their family rela-tionships. Only 8% of these youth would exclude Negroes

from the church (vs. 24%) and only one in five (20% vs. 54%) would condone premarital relationships. On the Religious Commitment scale these youth score in the upper end of the distribution.

Even if we include the fact that general religionists seem to care less about who climbs into bed with whom before marriage, I think it would be safe to say that their generalizing kind of morality, while it dulls conscience, cannot give them the specific sense of liberation which Christ's forgiven people know.

How many church youth have adopted religion-in-general as part of their everyday life? According to Dr. Strommen, in the most conservative Synod it would be two out of five, but in specific congregations it would often be one out of two.

In a survey of college-age Roman Catholics, Father Andrew Greeley found that a surprisingly large number of educated Catholics were loyal to the Church. But they found increasing difficulty in showing how their values as Catholics differed from those around them, and they found great difficulty in applying distinctive Christianity to their lives. Roy Fairchild and John Charles Wynn worked with active Presbyterian leadership families. They found loyalty to Christian institutions and a desire to see Christianity do some good in the community. But most of them adhered to religion-in-general, believing that beliefs mattered little and that after all most religions were about the same. Many went to church for sociability but only a few saw that their fellowship together was redeeming.

Victor Obenhaus and W. W. Schroeder have made impressive surveys of religion in the traditionally Protestant midwestern countryside. They found that loyal church members were able with only about 40 per cent accuracy to say anything distinctive about Christianity over against other religions. About the same percentage knew something of the difference between the Old and the New Testaments or could tell the story of the Good Samaritan. The better they could tell it, the less ready they were to apply it to their lives.

Joseph R. Washington, Jr., has found that American Negroes have had to develop a kind of parallel culture-religion, cut off from many of the traditions of Christianity by white suppressors. While their generalized religion takes on some distinctive features as we might expect it would, on the whole it serves purposes of Negro culture independent of distinctive Christianity. Gerhard Lenski and Ben Gaffin Associates, as reported by Father John L. Thomas, in separate studies found that the people they sampled thought of themselves as being religiously conventional and faithful. Religion played a big part in their lives. But as far as basic signals were concerned, these were called by the circles of acquaintances who already shared the beliefs of those sampled. Seldom did historic Christian standards cut into those existing beliefs. It would be wearying to continue the list. Religion-in-general reveals its effectiveness wherever we turn. It is widespread and inventive. While apparently serving as a bulwark against mere worldliness, it becomes the means by which worldliness modifies Christian teaching.

Once again, we have been implying that something is wrong with this rapidly spreading culture-religion. One could argue that it spreads because it is successful and that it is successful because it is good. What is wrong with it, specifically, from the Christian point of view?

A more formal look at an informal religion

THE DOCTRINES OF RELIGION-IN-GENERAL

Most religions can be approached doctrinally. That is, if you want to know what they are all about you ask what their doctrines and beliefs are. If you wanted to know about Christianity, you would pick up a book with chapter headings something like this:

> The Idea of God
> The Existence of God
> The Fact of Jesus
> The Incarnation
> The Natural Man
> The Doctrine of Sin
> The Nature of Salvation
> The Saving Work of Christ
> The Atonement
> The Holy Spirit
> The Trinity

The Church
The Sacraments
The Ministry
The Doctrine of Judgment
The Resurrection of the Body
The Second Coming

After you were familiar with these basic beliefs you would move on to study ways of worship, practices, ways of life.

We have had to move in the opposite direction for obvious reasons. Perhaps if American culture survives a thousand years it too will have codebooks and creeds for its national religion. (But not if Christians who care can help it!) At present such codes and creeds do not exist because religion-in-general has not needed them nor developed them. As a young and ... 'ng religion it remains less well-organized and its beliefs are not all systematic.

AN INFORMAL CREED

Still, like all complicated faiths, it has a creed, at least an informal one. One will find it best by beginning with common speech. Let me propose five completely haphazard sentences, any of which will put a person on the trail of someone who no doubt holds to other beliefs of generalized culture-religion. We are a long way from the formality of the Apostles' Creed or the Nicene Creed of Christianity, but they too no doubt got started in the market places or living rooms, where these sentences are usually spoken.

1. "Well, after all, in matters of religion the people of different faiths are just in different boats heading for the same shore."

2. "It does not make any difference what anybody believes, so long as he believes."

3. "I may not agree with his religion. But he's so sincere. That's all that matters."

4. "I don't really belong to the church. But I am very religious."

5. "I don't have a clear idea of Christian beliefs, but I am a Christian and I'm sure I believe in its main principles such as the Sermon on the Mount and the Golden Rule and the Ten Commandments."

What is wrong with these typical statements? On their own terms, as creeds or statements of generalized religion there is nothing at all wrong with them. They are quite exact statements of their own system. *They might even be true.* Our only measure is distinctive Christianity, by which those who speak them usually wish to be measured.

We can try a few quick questions and answers to meet the above questions:

1. Do you really believe that about the one shore and the many boats? Where did you learn it? Was it revealed to you, or can it be demonstrated or did you come to it by the process of reason? Where does Christianity clearly assert this?

2. Do you really believe that it makes no difference what any believer believes, so long as he is a believer? Do you believe that of the anarchist, or the Communist, or the Black Muslim, or the Moloch-worshiper who burned babies in sacrifice? If you rule out some of these as not fitting in, then you have begun to insert definitions. On what basis do you choose?

3. Is sincerity all that matters? The leaders of world Communism, which you profess to despise, may very well be most sincere.

4. I have no argument with you. You are very religious; that is apparent. Is there a similarity between religiousness and Christianity? Does Christianity allow for "not belonging to the church"? If so, show me how and where.

5. Every religion has a Golden Rule. There is not much that is original in the Ten Commandments or the Sermon on the Mount. What matters is who spoke them, and to whom, and with what purpose and setting.

Brother and sister, you have a discussion going.

A MORE FORMAL CREED

Actually, generalized religion in America tends to have somewhat more formal teachings than these paragraphs imply. We learn most about them if we see them in the context and setting in which they were developed, since there is little that is original in any of them. It is the whole, the complex that matters.

Like most religions, it has a *doctrine of God*. Culture-religion does not profess merely to worship man but to have an object outside itself. Usually this will be a national deity, one who relates best to my group. In any case, while he bears many features of the God of the previous religion, he will not in any way embarrass my group's way of life. This means that he is controllable; he makes his will clearly known and we are capable of following it. He punishes and he rewards.

There is a *doctrine of revelation*. The environment itself reveals and redeems. Being born in America, belonging to a favored group in America, making good use of its resources, using the book of nature and invention—in all of these ways I come to a knowledge of the deity's purposes. Certain basic national documents like Presidential inaugural addresses or the Declaration of Independence reveal much about this religion.

God has a *will* for the nation and it can without doubt be claimed by this nation. This intimate knowledge of the Almighty's purposes is most clear in war time, when our side is always right, and during political campaigns, when he identifies with our side.

There are doctrines of *creation and predestination*. I know that God planned this part of the creation and the world for people like me. We may have to keep some people out, but all decent people are welcome.

Providence and preservation are strong points. In the end, after some setbacks, God will see to it that everything turns out all right.

A *doctrine of man* is integral to any religion. Religion-in-general knows that man is or can be both good and bad, but asserts, "There is so much good in the worst of us, and so much bad in the best of us, that it ill behooves any of us to find fault with the rest of us." Of course we reserve the right to find fault with people who do not belong at all. Worst of all are those who resist our teachings and want to be distinctive.

There is a *covenant of works*. Man earns his salvation. Though God is good to bestow his gifts, basically he is impressed by what we have achieved and are achieving. He has merit badges which he hands out to the good. The undeserving are cast aside.

A *covenant of grace* appears. Man cannot do everything. He needs help. God can be consulted for such help. There are of course no atheists in foxholes.

The *doctrine of Christ* holds that he is the greatest man and maybe the Son of God; he is the Master and great teacher of our religion.

One can *repent* and be reborn or converted, if he is not too far from the central positions of the culture-religion. But if he is really alien, why does he not leave the country?

We have a *doctrine of fellowship*. All good people basically of our kind should come together. At least we should have good attitudes toward each other. The family that prays together stays together. I think that other races are all right in their place, and I may even be for racial integration without being excommunicated. Many good integrationists are active in religion-in-general.

There are *means of grace* and ceremonies: salutes to the flag, Presidential inaugural occasions, prayers at the service club are all meaningful opportunities for expression of our faith.

We do not talk much about death, but we honor the dead, who are probably rewarded in *the after life,* if there is an after life, which there probably is.

Et cetera.

RELIGION-IN-GENERAL'S BETTER PAST

I will be the first to admit that these are very informal, highly provocative, perhaps slightly pointed, but still not unfair summaries of central tenets of generalized religion. Whoever consults a member of the nationalist faction will receive much more important and certainly nobler versions of these statements. The business community can present hymns of success which are more compelling than some of these crabby and confining expressions. The mass media and Madison Avenue have their versions. I chose to try to capture the living-room sentiments which are major factors in American generalized religion. In some living rooms the creedal statements would be more distinctly Christian in their remembrance. In others the spokesman might trade on the memories of Judaism. Here and there one might learn a philosophical expression of such truths. In many other living rooms the statements might be even more drained of specific historic religious recall.

If it is necessary to be *doctrinally* severe with religion-in-general in the interest of Christian identity, one may be more generous with such a religion *historically*. Here matters grow more complicated. For this religion seems to be clearly superior to most of the alternatives which could have grown up. In some respects, it certainly has a better record than Christianity before it had. One does not need much imagination or memory to see how much worse off Americans would have been had their nation developed an ugly, authoritarian, exclusivist, intolerant, fanatic religion.

WHAT AMERICA NEEDED

America needed a *universalist* religion because its particular ones made competitive claims and were not capable of bringing unity to the new society. If Americans have been uncharitable to non-Americans or un-Americans; if they have often been prejudicial and have welcomed newcomers with less than full enthusiasm, at least things would have been worse if a severe doctrine had defined the new nation.

When the new nation developed it was natural and perhaps necessary that its broad religion should be *"syncretistic."* That means, it was natural that with people of so many religious backgrounds in a new environment, their religions should begin to get mixed up with each other. They improvised on the basis of these. Just as understandably, there was a natural tendency toward *relativism*, the teaching that implies that almost everything is equally true with everything else—or equally false. *Tolerance* did not come easily, but it came to people whose basic charter, written during the Enlightenment period, declared that men were indeed created equal. If generalized religion is *moralistic*, this too is understandable (and better than if it had been immoralistic). Americans may thus be hypocritical at times and petty at others, but one can understand that they expected their traditional religions and their emerging religion to produce good men and women. And if religion-in-general was *materialist,* offering more good things than true meanings, what in America did not tend to do this?

American institutions grew out of a practical solution: many different religious groups competed; none could prevail by itself. The philosophy of the Enlightenment worked toward a natural religion to which all men could assent. The optimism built into Americans as things worked for them and as they found ever new resources made its contribution.

Religion-in-general, then, was a logical outgrowth in American history. It has many attractive features. No Christian or Jew would probably want to see its every feature killed off. But he will have to make up his mind about the basis of this generalized religion in the light of his specific views about God, man, and destiny. It may be better than Christianity, and will either displace or improve Christianity. Unquestionably it has helped produce a more tolerant Christian community, and it has made other contributions to the churches. If it is not better than Christianity, it may be the same thing in a different translation. It may be an exact parallel, in which case the two are compatible and there is no conflict. This book suggests that this alternative is not defensible. Or it may be worse than and a detriment to Christian faith. Most Americans drift casually between Christianity and religion-in-general. The excitements in our history have come in confrontations between those who witness to distinctive Christianity and those who think that America needs a better religion based, perhaps, on Christianity but one which is acceptable to all and which has no exclusive features.

A LIFE LIVED WITH GENERAL RELIGIONISTS

The purist may wonder whether America's religion-in-general is escapable. Yes. One can be a monk or a nun or a hermit in relation to it. He can find a salt mine and hide there, or build a pillar and get up on it. (In either case he will become a curiosity and then a success; thus he will be a good man and soon another national saint.) He can be a complete sectarian and withdraw from the society into an obscure colony somewhere. But he is probably not given any of these alternatives if he is a Christian, and therefore called to praise and serve God at the side of Jesus Christ in the middle of the world and in the middle of the city.

Most of us, therefore, will not escape religion-in-general even if we mildly try. We shall confront it all our lives, since it shows no signs of completely dying out.

Religion-in-general will meet us as young people in "bull sessions" or locker-room chats. Now and then we turn to serious conversation. People who do not know too much about Christian doctrine will lapse into generalized religious talk. Those who desire to please everybody resort to it, because it cannot possibly offend any one. We shall meet it in living rooms, where we use it to fight off the missionary-minded ministerial guest or to satisfy ourselves.

Americans meet religion-in-general in its more ceremonial forms in public schools, lodges, service clubs, and fraternities. Few of these are devised without some sort of religious base, and seldom will that base be precisely the same thing as distinctive Christianity. Generalized religion was incarnate in the little twenty-two-word prayer which the New York Board of Regents manufactured for school children, and which some New York schools used until the United States Supreme Court prohibited it in 1962. (The

Supreme Court has been in trouble with some sectors of the population in the past decade because it has seen that religion-in-general is a specific faith which should not be established in public institutions.)

Political leaders and sometimes Presidents are the best national spokesmen for the common faith and its mystique. Mass communicators, knowing that competitive religions are present in their audiences, more often than not will trim the cutting edges of religious witness to cater to the majority. We confront generalized religion on billboards and in newspaper editorials. Religion-in-general is not infrequently established in the churches themselves. More often than not it is the undeclared religion of lay leaders; sometimes a minister believes in it or seeks to gain favor with its adherents.

Generalized religion has been at its best when it has been most infused by particular Christianity. The best example is found in Abraham Lincoln. His devotion to the Union was almost mystical and could have been idolatrous. But, though he was not an orthodox Christian, he was informed by the Bible and by historic Protestantism's witness to the fact that God keeps His own counsels, that He judges nations and men, that His purposes and ours may clash, and that we had better seek to be on His side than to claim Him on ours. The symbolic power of the best side of generalized national religion (I am tempted to say the *necessary* aspect, if there is to be a nation) is evident, for example, at the Tomb of the Unknown Soldier or at a burial of a President. Its weakest side is present in the little contrived witnesses such as in the politically motivated religious words on coins and in national pledges.

I have not dealt with the problem of generalized religion when it does become too clear, too specific. What if it becomes an ideology, a doctrine which serves to justify a purpose or program? What if it has the field to itself, without competition, without judgment? We receive ugly glimpses of this when extremist movements camp on everything that can be called American or nationalist or religious and try to force all to accept their definitions. If Christians withdraw in fear and refuse to enter the public arena, they will abandon the broad features of national life to the dogmatists of national generalized religion. The record of such dogmatists' achievements in Germany and elsewhere should give Christians good reason to stay very much in the middle of things and to do their arguing or make their contributions out of the center of their tradition.

How can Christians stand apart?

DISTINCTIVE CHRISTIANITY AND GENERAL RELIGION

The adjective "distinctive" has been attached to the word Christian again and again in this book. The word "particular" might have done as well; anything which sets Christianity apart is seen as a barrier against the overpowering embrace of culture-religion. It is unfair to move from this subject without doing some justice to the problem of distinctiveness. Is criticism of religion-in-general merely clubby? May not Christianity become a kind of elite corps of tired aristocrats? Will not the loving purpose of God be defeated if Christians set themselves apart?

Many intelligent, informed and concerned people in the world have found good reason to suggest that whenever Christians are concerned with their own identity they become prideful. It would be hazardous to forget or to slight that history. On the other hand, it is possible to set Christian distinctiveness into context.

The first reply that comes to mind is this: Christianity wants to be a universal faith. It asserts that Christ died for all. It takes momentum from the cross and wants to spread like contagion through all the world. It believes that Jesus is "the true light that enlightens every man" (Jn. 1:9). If so, no one can claim Jesus just for himself or his club. The followers of Jesus believe that "there is salvation in no one else, for there is no other name under heaven given among men by which we must be saved" (Acts 4:12). But they want to see the power of that name at work even where it is not recognized. In Christ "all things hold together" (Col. 1:17). In the more aggressive sense, Christians want to go into all the world to make disciples. In their healthier moments and eras they have not tried to be a club concerned only about themselves.

These universal concerns of Christianity are not satisfying to the general religionist. He is not sure that any one can die for any one else. He does not recognize the light uniquely in Jesus Christ. He thinks the world holds itself together, or at least does not need Christ. He thinks that the missionary command of Jesus does not deal with the realities of world religion. He wants a religion that is immediately accessible to everyone, at least inside his own culture. Nothing particular or distinctive will do, he says, not noting how private and unique his own faith is.

The general religionist believes that he, and not the Christian, serves God and man better by contributing to "the emerging religion of the species" which will unite and attract all men. He would eliminate religious conflict and would produce fulfillment and human concord. He is the really tolerant man and thus he better enacts Christian love toward the neighbor. And his system works.

Actually, we are here giving him too much credit. Advocates of religion-in-general very often are much devoted to one tiny segment of humanity: the prosperous and productive American middle class. So long as any one can meet its terms all is well. If someone does not, he is not understood or even noticed. They resent nothing more than the forms of Christianity which ask them to keep all men, the whole world, in view. But at its best, are there good prospects if Christianity were to merge with generalized religion and lose its separate identity?

Such a merger could come by natural development. National religion could become international. The Universal Declaration of the Rights of Man could provide a base for Christian relations to a world-wide religion-in-general. In a world which is often anti-God, all kinds of believers are often finding it profitable to stick together. Perhaps they will find themselves really sticking together.

Such a merger could grow out of the Christian ecumenical movement and the American interfaith movement. But such a process is slow and painful. So the general-religion group argues that more can be done. The spiritual fitting-together of the world should be entrusted to them. Such a vision of an integrated, coherent, fit-together humanity has its attractions. It sounds like the Christian ideal.

The Christian asks questions. Is the general religionist's proposal based on truth? If so, the Christian has to accept it; if not, he dare not. This question of truth is seldom taken seriously in our cultural-religious climate. But if we really care about a person's integrity and humanity or his fulfillment, we must begin by letting him be and remain what he is, if there his commitment to truth is to be found.

The second Christian question: is absorption into general religion advisable? Can one do it and be faithful to Jesus' call to be disciples, to follow Him? Are the values of general religion demonstrably better? Are there not embarrassments in its history? Third, what are the prospects? Christianity may be distinctive and private, in the eyes of many. But it cuts across racial and national grounds. It was born in the East and thrives in the West while enduring in the East. It is the language of faith somewhere or other in the majority of the nations of the world. One need not be found in a certain set of circumstances to find meaning from it.

Could it be that the "universalists" are the really private group? Whenever someone stands up and says, "Let me devise the religion that will integrate the world," watch him. He will sell a few books and gain some adherents. But his system will, in the eyes of the larger circle of humanity, be more mysterious and private than the "particular" systems he would displace. America's religion-in-general is not universal at all. Most of its features would be incomprehensible to people with any other national history and with a different basic set of experiences. We think it is acceptable for the same reasons that each of us feels at home in "our own darkness" where all is familiar. But we are frightened or bewildered in unfamiliar darkness.

The advocate of religion-in-general will continue to be popular. He says what the society wants to hear and says it simply. One is not called to anything really difficult and demanding by it. It has always appealed to Americans who wanted to leave behind the pettiness of European Christianity in centuries past. It helps people find security in the insecurity of American religious competition. It is an effective base for many kinds of national action. But to the adherents of the other religions of the world it is private and it speaks to itself. Christians, while they seek better ways of disciplining themselves and speaking to others, already have a faith which can help unite men or can help serve men before they are united.

The difficult questions for young Christians

THE QUESTIONS WE MUST FACE

Young Christians will no doubt grow up in a climate in which religion-in-general and a number of other faiths will compete with Christianity for attention. In such a world they will do well to think through an adult set of attitudes.

Most important is that they begin to learn to identify alternatives to the Christian faith. The motive for this work is neither to prepare persons to be snoops concerning other people's opinions nor to make them better debaters. It is to equip Christians to make important decisions. After they can identify cultural alternatives to faith, they can decide what to do about them. Certain features are compatible: they provide opportunities for mutual service. Certain features undercut the faith: they must be recognized and fought off.

The spirit of such a confrontation is important. What

could be less attractive than if Christians were merely prissy in their quest for exact definition? What could be less fruitful than if Christians became the "mim" people, the religious disapprovers who had no positive approach to life? So much of religion-in-general is based on a relaxed defense of the existing way of life or of the supposed "good old days" which preceded it. Where is there room in it for the kind of improbable actions through which a world is changed and a Christ served? Cantankerousness, withdrawal, pettiness, lovelessness, dowdiness—none of these will serve the Christian cause.

THE LEGITIMATE QUESTIONS

When Christians ask questions of their contemporaries who hold to religion-in-general, they will be careful not to place Christian truth on the cafeteria line and debate its superiority. Christianity is not and does not want to be a superior religion. "Superior" means that we come at people from above and look down on them. Jesus asks for people to minister, to serve, to come from below. Christianity is not a systematic attempt to provide the best answers; that is not its truth. Christianity seeks to bear witness to Jesus Christ who calls Himself the truth.

The Christian's second legitimate question will be ethical. While he admits all the faults of Christians in the realm of good works, he can ask: does religion-in-general have a motivating, an energizing, a generating center out of which goodness flows? What or who judges generalized religion for its failures? What or who calls it into a reconciling circle? What in it really frees one for service?

The third question about culture-religion is, What are its fruits? Can it produce people of profound character? Has it missionaries? Or does it content itself with calling together people who are in on inventing it, or who are naturally inclined to it? Does it notice its own temptations to pride, the ways in which it tries to exempt itself from criticism?

Christians will also ask, What is in it for us? They need not ask this in the merely selfish sense. Rather, what elements in our religious environment will help us better serve, better spread the love of God? Certainly religion-in-general is a kind of judgment on meaningless Christian divisions. It reminds Christians that they are to relate to all that is around them. Sometimes culture-religion may be a partner and not merely a threat to faith. Religion-in-general, like many other problems facing the Church, can be an instrument for renewal. It can prod Christians toward reunion. It can cause them to revise their unlovely mannerisms. It can force them to keep their thinking clear and fresh. It can call forth a less muffled witness. It can challenge Christians to produce the works of love in society.

The presence of religion-in-general presents young Christians with two really basic difficulties. The first has to do with the judgment faith makes on religion; the second deals with the question of truth and salvation in other religions.

A JUDGMENT ON RELIGION

Those who speak for Christian faith and Christian theology, even if their expression is well-mannered, must pronounce a judgment upon man's religions. On what grounds do they do so? To say that man's religion is a problem for authentic faith seems shocking to us today. Actually, little is at stake in the word "religion." It hardly occurs in the Bible and is seldom related to the faith when that faith is vital.

Jesus spent most of his ministry fighting religion. A reading of the Gospel reveals that Jesus spent little energy on

atheism and only a little more on agnosticism. Neither of
these seemed to be around in the forms we recognize. He
did fight apathy. But most of his work of releasing God's
loving power among men was hindered by religious leaders.
They were custodians of a religion-in-general which had a
Jewish reminiscence. He made it clear that religion was
closed to God's commands and promises. Man who had a
religion did not have ears to hear. He asked the best religionists of his day to be born again.

The apostles moved on a terrain rich with culture-religion; both the memory of Greece and the presence of Rome
worked to create a kind of worldly religiousness much like
that which we know today. St. Paul once or twice tried to
"hook in" on the people's existing religion. More often he
fought off the Jewish religious prerequisite, circumcision,
or the Roman requirement, devotion to the emperor.

The Protestant Reformers saw the danger in religion. It
could produce the *bonus vir,* the good man; it could produce *justitia civilis,* a righteousness in civil society. It could
not make man open to God. Two centuries later religion
really came into its own in the period of the Enlightenment.
The word appealed to those who stressed what man could
naturally and by reason do. Today we are involved in a
great attempt to extricate Christianity from the static and
suffocating bonds of religion.

Some Christian thinkers of our time have come to speak
of religion as "unbelief," as what man does to keep God
from speaking to him. When God reveals Himself He must
first shatter our generalized religion. He meets us in ways
our religion did not train us to expect. Religion is basically
man's faith in himself, with God as an extra added attraction. Faith depends upon God to create something new in
us. Christian faith easily comes to be a religion too. In each

generation prophets and protestants have to shake it loose from its own religiousness.

While Christianity shatters man's generalized religion, even this important act of shattering must be done in a proper spirit. The Christian can look prideful and arrogant; he can appear to lack understanding. But he can so cut himself off from the thinking people of a culture that they will not understand him. Better: a much broader corps of informed and thoughtful Christian laymen than we have had in the past can serve to "telegraph the shots" of the Church to the world. They can show that Christians have a lovers' quarrel with the world. But it is a lovers' quarrel. They really want to speak to the culture and see it redeemed.

A MOST DIFFICULT QUESTION

The second question has less to do with technique or definition. It relates to one of the most difficult topics in the whole book of the faith. If Christian faith is to judge and extricate itself from religion-in-general, what about the truth that is found in the rejected religion? We usually see this question asked concerning the people who are never confronted with Christianity. "What happens to the unbaptized heathen?" "What about the people who never heard?" "What about people in Hindu culture who never had a chance to escape and take a critical inquiring look at Jesus Christ? What if they are good Hindus, and they show their love to God and man?" Now this set of questions should be applied to those inside a once-Christian culture who know but apparently do not need Jesus Christ. What about the truth and destiny of such people?

I am almost overcome by my overpowering sense of modesty at this point. Let there be no false advertising. You will not receive an answer to this set of questions. You will only hear comment on the questions and clues to the answers. Anyone who seeks to give authoritative answers has to speak for God.

Christian faith exists to spread salvation. Salvation comes from a Hebrew root word, *'yasha,* which has many ideas implicit in it. To "be saved" meant to be given a large place, room to breathe, health and wholeness and freedom. This salvation is to transform life in the world. But "the world" does not exhaust the purposes of God. "Heaven," "eternal life," "the Kingdom of God" or "resurrection" are the words Christians use to witness to the fact that God's purposes are not confined to my today. The believer in religion-in-general does not have salvation, in that he must always defend his place, must always gasp for air, must always point to his achievements; he is not free to accept what God gives him. *What about his ultimate destiny?* This is where Christians who have a vivid sense of a future life like to locate the question.

If the question is asked, the young Christian has several things to say. First, he must remark that it is a legitimate and understandable question. It may be motivated by real love for others. It will grow out of a seriousness about man and a view of God which does God honor: it recognizes God's loving purpose. It is based on an understanding of Christian failure: how can believers be so relaxed, so mindless about religion-in-general, if they know so much about the dire fate of *its* believers?

More can be said. A young Christian should, secondly, ask his questioner to locate the question at the right place. If it is merely an academic debating point, a "tease" question, the Bible and the Christian tradition are of no help and the discussion makes something very important turn out to be very trivial. But if the question is "existentially" put so that it involves a person's sense of destiny, it should be faced eagerly. Where is the question to be located? Not at the beginning of a religious discussion but at the end; not at the beginning of a quest for faith and love but at the end.

If the question comes at the beginning it is a lazy question; it takes the whole sap out of the life's work. At the end of his quest for learning a Faust can say, "I now do know that we do nothing know." But that would hardly do as a motto under a freshman's desk glass. A jungle doctor at the end of his life can say, "It almost seems fruitless; one makes such a small gain against human misery." But if he begins his career that way he will make no gains at all.

If a person hears Christian witness with a religious man's ear; if he listens out of curiosity about the cleverness of the speaker while all along he knows the answer (all religion is good; all religions are really the same), he will not undertake Christian discipleship. If he takes the revelation which has been given him with utter moral and theological seriousness, he can one day realize the meaning of grace in a vivid sense. At the end of the day, as an unprofitable servant he can realize what he did not achieve himself. But he will have extended himself for others, trying to reach and to serve them. *Then,* as he "turns things wholly back to God again," as it were, he can face the questions about those whom he did not reach or who did not understand.

Third, the Christian has to be sure that his answers do not sentimentalize life. The Christian revelation knows condemnation. Not everything always turns out right in the end. Perhaps W. H. Auden is correct: no one is ever sent to hell, men simply go there. But it is clear that a man can turn his back on God's large place, on health and wholeness and salvation. A man can harden his heart and thus thwart God's purposes which were to be worked through him.

More: he can say that in the Christian witness, whoever is saved is saved in Christ. How this is or can be, or how it is extended and worked out, he has but few faint ideas. But nothing he can say should distract from the cosmic or universal purpose or necessity of Christ's words and works. If he can devise a way around Christ, let him take it. Let him then see that Christ's sacrifice was foolish because it was unnecessary.

A thoughtful Christian will not want to let the questioner leave him without hearing a Christian confession of honest regret for the past sins of "distinctive" and particular Christians. They have used the sword and they have used force in order to prevail. We cannot share the joys of Christian tradition without inheriting the burdens. We must see what we owe the world, also in penance, and do our generation's part to see that mistakes are not repeated and that the past is atoned for.

But the same thoughtful Christian can also show that the more general religion is not automatically the more tolerant and the more particular automatically the less tolerant. In our world the opposite seems often to be the case. Religion-in-general produces a kind of tolerance which often does not wear well when tested. People of profound convictions and commitments based on faith are less insecure, less fearful; they can be more free to understand and to work creatively with those with whom they do not agree. Is it really demonstrable that religion-in-general is so tolerant?

Finally, Christians can say that they have no choice but to work with the revelation given them. If they exhaust the depth of God's truth in Jesus Christ, then they will look for it elsewhere. If they have been able to do better than to live by faith in Him, they live a lie if they do not move on from this distinctive point into the broad general ones. In the meantime the Christian has riches whose depth he has not reached. If he carries on a mission to the world, he does it not to exploit persons but to present Christ to them. If he serves, it will not be for the glory of the Church but because of the need of man.

AN UNFAMILIAR TASK

No one need pretend that he has not been put through a wringer by these pages. We have been asked to look at religion in what may seem to be a wholly unfamiliar way. We have not used the words we used in primary Sunday School. We have used words which match the level of the science and history of our high school years; some of the ideas may have been more complex than we are accustomed to. Without doubt, our attempt to cover such a large topic in so little space has led to some obscurity. Hardest of all, we have been asked to make basic decisions about the environment. We are asked to deny certain popular elements in it. But if at any place there has been a hint that the Christian faith is less liberating, less joyous than religion-in-general, the false hint is the fault of the writer.

I wish I could sidle up to a young people's discussion group as it relates to religion-in-general. Were I old enough so that the line could come with better grace, I would have one good Protestant word to whisper. The whole book has been a development of this theme: "Little children, keep yourselves from idols" (I Jn. 5:21).

BER

BON

BROV

COHE

HUDS

JENKI

LEWI

McL

NICH

WALS

DATE DUE   BORROWER'S NAME

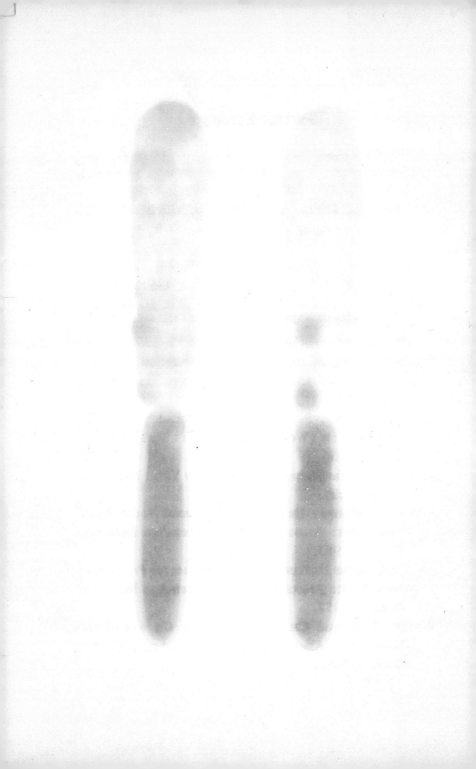